Jean Wright is a retired primary school teacher specialising in Geography, Environmental Studies, Local and Family History. She is Bollington born and bred and still lives there. A lifelong member of Bollington Methodist Church, she has been its archivist since 1976.

Jean has enjoyed many local groups and Adult Education classes. She has worked with local history groups for the first Bollington Festival in 1964 and in the Bollington Civic Society Photographic Archive. Her 1963 tape recording of 96 year old Grandma Martha Ann Wright used in the Festival Exhibition was instrumental in researching the family history in 1974. She was later requested to write "Martha Ann's Story" for use in the Victorian Schoolroom in the Silk Heritage Centre. A WEA/Manchester University Extra Mural Department Genealogy Course resulted in writing "The Underhill Family of Macclesfield". A former member of Macclesfield Historical Society and both Cheshire Family History Societies, she wrote articles for "North Cheshire Family Historian" magazine. Since inheriting an extensive collection of rare original family letters and photographs, it has been Jean's wish both to share them with others, and to ensure their long term conservation at Macclesfield Silk Heritage Museum for artefacts and Cheshire Record Office for papers. "Voices from the Past" 2005 links together the original letters and photographs with relevant background information.

Dedication

This book is dedicated to Martha Ann Wright, whose voice from the past has been its inspiration

---

First Published 2005 by
Wright Publications
1A Hall Hill
Bollington
Macclesfield
Cheshire
SK10 5ED

Jean M Wright

Printed by Franklyn Publicity

Contents

Preface and Acknowledgements to
"Letters from a Lady's Maid"

Grandma Martha Ann Wright first told me that her mother Ann (nee Bennett) had been Lady's Maid to Miss Agnes Greg at The Mount, Bollington, when we were naming photographs in her Victorian album. Grandma Wright had many vivid memories of her long life of over 100 years. She knew the Greg family and had lived at Lowerhouse in the 1880's. Her recollections are included, together with information on Samuel Greg, junior, and his model village.

In preparation for the Historical Exhibition of the first Bollington Festival, September 1964, I tape recorded Martha Ann's early memories. Visitors to the Historical Exhibition marquee could hear them played, as they saw her rose coloured silk poplin wedding dress and wedding photo on display. (Later donated, with other relevant family antiques, to Macclesfield Silk Hertiage Museum) Martha Ann's memories were the inspiration for my family history research from 1975 onwards. In December 1978 we 'found' Ann Bennett's original letters, with her daguerrotype, and items from her chatelaine in the 'secret' drawer inside the family oak chest we had inherited. Exciting tangible links with our lady's maid great grandma! Photographs of some of her needlework tools are shown in colour.

Major life changes followed. Living alone, I joined creative classes on watercolours, creative embroidery and antiques. Chronic M.E. was diagnosed and there were major relapses with basic survival. When the Antiques Roadshow visited Macclesfield, one of the staff advised me to try to publish these rare original letters. In 1991 I was struggling to write down "Martha Ann's Story" for my grandsons and for use in the Victorian Schoolroom of the Education Department of Macclesfield Silk Heritage Centre. It was produced thanks to the help of Molly Spink and staff there. Further major relapses occurred and I had to wait for remissions. In Summer 2002 Gill Parry scripted Ann's letters and scanned family photographs onto computer. Background information was needed so that they could be better understood. Gwyneth Mitchell advised and confirmed their rarity as primary source material. Adam Daber, curator at Quarry Bank Mill, Styal, provided information from their archives about Samuel Greg, junior, and Lowerhouse Mill. Friends in Macclesfield Embroiderers Guild lent books and the curator at Gawthorpe Hall, Lorna Rogerson, recommended books on Needlework Tools. Hazel Weselby has put written information onto computer. Her husband, Jim Weselby, photographed Ann Bennett's sewing box, needlework tools and samples. Gill and Hazel added captions to photographs.

Sincere thanks to all these people and especially to Gill, Hazel and Jim who willingly have given their time and pivotal computer skills and to everyone who has encouraged and willingly given time and practical help. It is a miracle that together they have enabled this rare, original source material to be put together in book form so that others may share and enjoy this 'time capsule' of a lady's maid.

Preface for "Voices from the Past"

"Voices from the Past" has evolved since publishing a limited number of copies of "Letters from a Lady's Maid" in 2003. It was suggested that the book should be rewritten to combine together all the additional family letters and documents which had recently come to light.

It is remarkable that this rare collection of original material has survived intact for almost 175 years, thanks to being cared for by generations of family members. These fragile papers are to be deposited at Cheshire Record Office in safekeeping for others to share.

The original handwritten letters and papers have been transcribed here for easier reading, while retaining the original spelling. Background information throws light on the letters and photographs. It is social history in the words of the people themselves, shown on a family tree extract next to the back cover.

It has been my privilege and calling to share a treasured family collection to link past and present together so that others may have the opportunity to 'hear their voices'.

Jean M Wright
Bollington
May 2005

1

Ann Bennett's Early Life

First, an introduction to Ann Bennett and her family. From family history research, we know that Ann Bennett was born on the 19 February 1838 (Birth Certificate) at Pott Shrigley. She was the younger daughter of Charles Bennett and Jane (nee Underhill). Her elder sister, Mary, was born before Civil Registration began in 1837. Both daughters were baptised at St. Michaels Church, Macclesfield, where their parents were married in 1834. (The Underhill family attended St. Michaels Parish Church) Mary was baptised on 20 September 1835 and Ann on 8 April 1838.

We have further information about the family from the Census Returns. On the night of 7 June 1841, the Census records that Jane Bennett (nee Underhill), aged 32, with her daughters Mary, 5, and Ann, 3, were staying with Jane's eldest brother, John Underhill and his wife, Betty. They were owners and publicans at the Cross Keys Hotel, Macclesfield. The Cross Keys Hotel was situated on an island in the road next to Arighi's workshop between the 101 steps and Macclesfield railway station.
The Underhill family were well respected Macclesfield builders during the Industrial Revolution.

By the 1851 census, Charles Bennett, aged 43, and Jane, aged 41, were living at Hope Green, Adlington. Charles was a railway platelayer. A railway platelayer was at the forefront of the modern technology of the day. Jane's occupation was schoolmistress. Mary was aged 15 and Ann 13 years old. Ann was given useful books of crochet work patterns (1851) and Girls Own Book (1857) shown. Ann, aged 15 years, received a Valentine card and suitor's letter dated 20 January 1853, from James Clayton Fletcher of Poynton Village, near Stockport. About 1853, Ann's portrait was taken to mark an important rite of passage like her apprenticeship. In the 1850's portraiture used the daguerreotype process. For protection Ann's portrait is framed inside a small folding leather case, fastened with a gold hook, see illustration in the colour plates.

For Victorian times, Mary and Ann were well-educated girls. They helped their mother Jane to run the home. They learnt how to bake bread and biscuits and cook on an open coal fire, and do cleaning, washing and ironing. Scripted examples of some handwritten family recipes are given in Chapter 2. Ann's daughter, Martha Ann Wright, described how her grandparents, Jane and Charles Bennett of Hope Green, drank herb teas made from hyssop, horehound and rosehips during the week. On Sundays, they drank expensive Indian or China tea, which was stored in small quantities in a locked wooden tea caddy. Tea was served in small patterned china tea bowls with matching dish shaped saucers. Mary and Ann were also accomplished needlewomen and embroiderers. Photographs show their dresses with handmade crochet lace collars and cuffs, and details of sampler motifs, Berlin work and needlework tools. Two of their Berlin work pictures on religious themes, were donated to the Macclesfield Silk Heritage Centre collection.

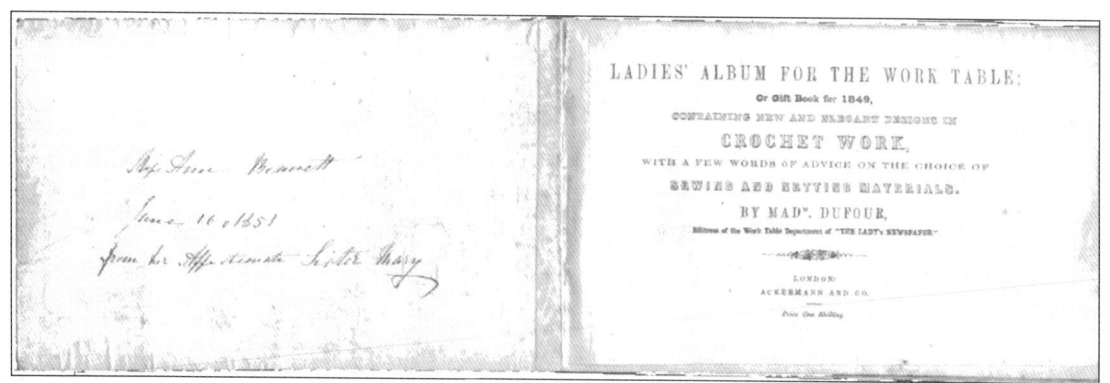

"a gift from her affectionate sister Mary, June 16 1851

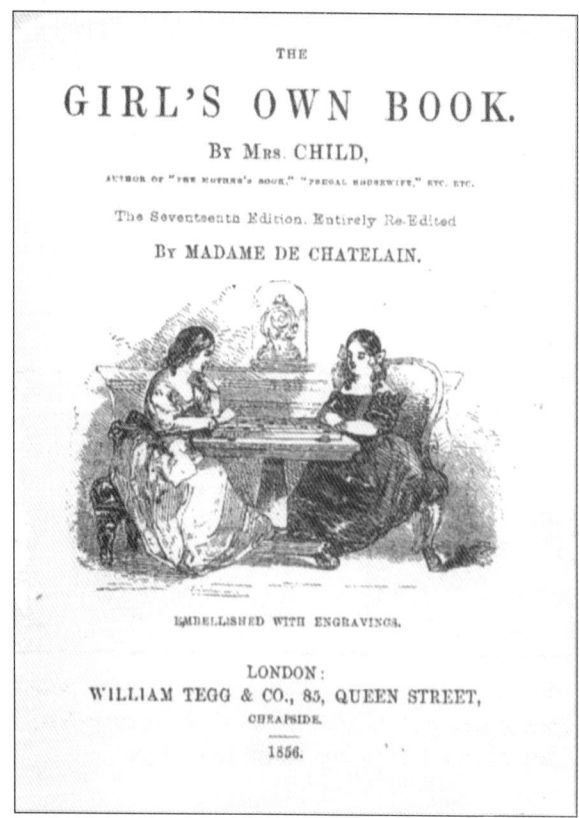

Ann Bennett signed and dated, 1857, her well used "Girls Own Book". It is full of ideas and instructions for games, exercises, charades, rhymes, riddles, poems, needlework, knitting, crochet, tatting, netting, keeping bees, gardening and letter writing.

Jane Bennett with her letter and spectacles

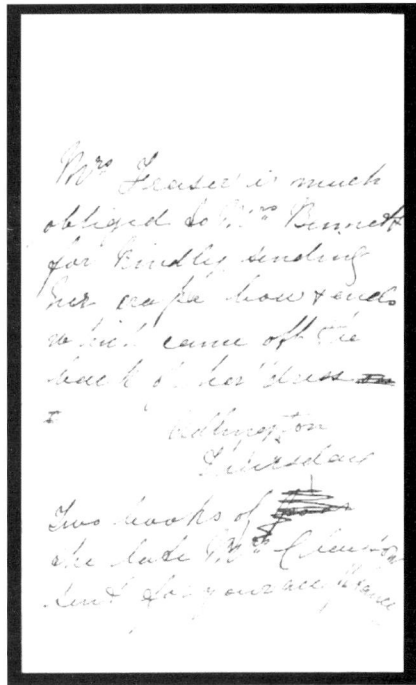

Jane Bennett (nee Underhill) wearing a black satin dress with lace collar, cuffs and cap

After Mrs. Clayton's funeral, Jane Bennett had returned Mrs. Fraser's "crepe bow and ends which came off the back of her dress" (probably removed to make it more comfortable to sit). It seems that these items were fastened onto a black dress to adapt it temporarily into suitable mourning wear for the funeral of a friend or neighbour.

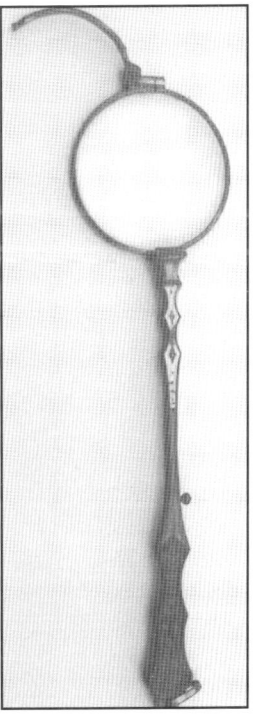

Part lorgnette with spring nose-bridge. Frame is 9 carat gold with royal blue and white enamelled decoration on the handle. Ring at the end for hanging chain/cord.

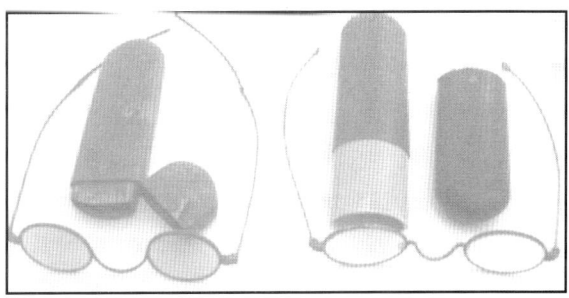

Metal framed spectacles with cardboard cases. Blue glass lenses with hinged sides to fit in the case (left). Clear glass lenses fit into longer case (right).

Jane Bennett, their mother, received a thank you letter from Mrs Fraser written on black edged notepaper in matching envelope. Following Mrs Clayton's funeral, Ann had returned Mrs Fraser's "bows and ends which came of the back of her dress". These were used to temporarily adapt an ordinary black dress to wear at a friend's funeral. The depth of mourning and time worn depended on the closeness of the relationship to the deceased. When a husband died, his widow wore black bombazine and widow's cap for one year and one month. In the last three months, jet jewellery and ribbons could be added.

Ann Bennett told her daughter, Martha Ann Wright, the story of how she became the only witness in a murder case. One day, when travelling by train to Macclesfield, she sat in the same carriage as a roughly dressed workman and a young lady carrying a fisherman's basket. Ann saw them both get off the train and noticed that the workman was following the girl. When returning home later that day, Ann arrived at Macclesfield station. The workman was waiting on the platform for the same train, with the girl's basket in his possession. Ann thought this was strange and told the police. Later the police found the girl's body on the canalside. The workman said he thought she might have some food in it, and so he murdered her. The judge highly commended Ann on her observation and astuteness.

In the late 1850's we know that Ann was apprenticed to Miss Dunnington, who was a dressmaker and milliner of Cumberland Street, Macclesfield. (Miss Dunnington is listed in the Trade Directories of 1857 and 1859). Ann would walk to work on Monday mornings and return home on Saturday evenings. During bad weather she travelled by train between Adlington/Poynton and Macclesfield. There Ann would learn many skills useful for her later employment. Mary Bennett became a servant, working in Stockport.

By her 4 February 1860 letter, Ann became lady's maid to Miss Agnes Greg, who had come from Quarrybank House, Styal in 1851 to live at The Mount, to help her brother Samuel's family after he took early retirement because of ill health. The Mount was divided into two households, so Miss Agnes (then aged 54 years) lived separately from the young family. Ann wrote letters to her mother and sister from The Mount and when she travelled with Miss Agnes to the seaside or to stay with Greg family members.

In the 1861 census for The Mount, Bollington, Ann is listed as a servant, aged 23. Samuel's elder brother, John Greg, was visiting The Mount. He lived at Caton, near Lancaster, and was Deputy Mayor of Lancaster and a Magistrate. At this time John was managing Lowerhouse Mill with his son, Francis.

Ann Bennett married Alfred Wright (joiner at Lowerhouse Mill) on 22 December 1864 at Prestbury Church. They lived in a cottage at the bottom of Flash (Bench) Lane (1871 census), in the corner of Samuel Greg's land near the Bollington boundary with Butley (added to the Tithe Map). Mary Bennett came to their home to help Ann with the children when Philip was born in 1871. When their parents Charles and Jane Bennett needed more care, Mary helped and returned home to Hope Green, Adlington. Uncle Thomas Underhill (Jane's brother) went to live at Hope Green, when he was unable to live alone in the cottage built by his father in Waterloo Street, Hurdsfield, which Mary and Ann later inherited. Charles Wright, aged 9 years stayed with Aunt Mary and grandparents at Hope Green when he attended school in Lostock Terrace, Poynton about 1874.

Mary was executor of Aunt Phoebe's will. Mary's account book for 1884 contains costs of her aunt's funeral and signatures of beneficiaries. Living alone, Mary kept accounts of her frugal expenditure. Later she lived in Beeston Mount, Bollington where she bought basic groceries from her niece Martha Ann and Richard Wright's shop at 13 - 15 Shrigley Road.

Thomas Underhill, Jan. 7th 1795 – Jan. 3rd 1879

Thomas Underhill, Scholar at Macclesfield Sunday School. Certificate for regular attendance.

Thomas Underhill, "nobbler" (school beadle), wearing his uniform. Photograph by Bullock, Macclesfield – about 1860.

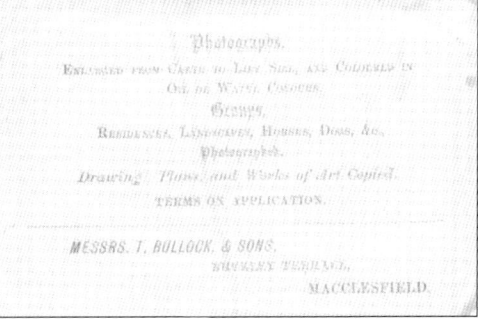

Thomas' Memorial Card

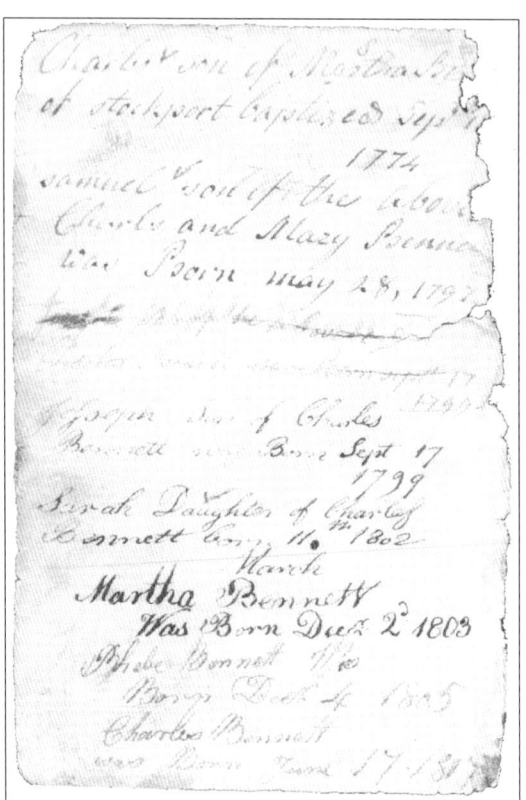

Sarah Bennett, born March 14th 1802 died October 12th 1866. This photograph was taken from a glass plate.

This page from the Bennett Family Bible records their births. Charles Bennett's sisters, Sarah and Phoebe, are both mentioned in Ann Bennett's letter to her sister Mary, written February 12th 1860, when uncle George died. They both lived at Skellorn Green, Adlington.

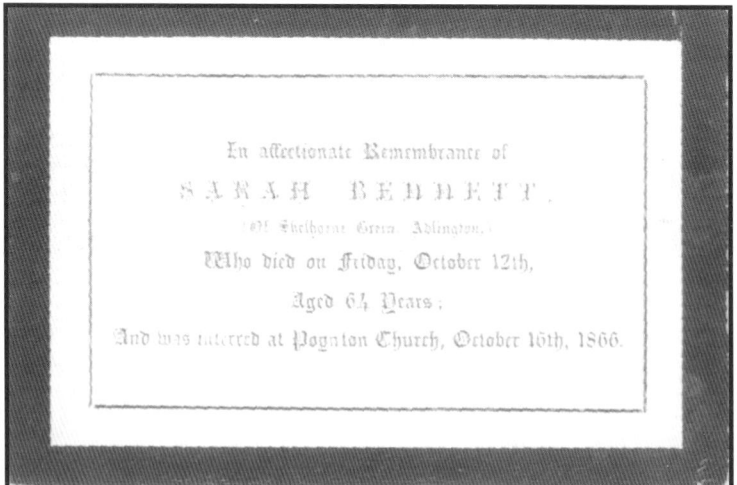

Sarah Bennett's memorial card

Charles & Jane Bennett (nee Underhill) of Hope Green, Adlington, parents of Mary and Ann. The Underhill Family Bible page records "Jane Underhill Born November 17 in the year of our Lord 1809 about $^1/_2$ past 2 in the afternoon, Married 1834, Died November 23rd 1876. Her husband Charles Bennett died August 3rd 1878 aged 70 years" (actually 71 years).

Their memorial cards give further details.

Phoebe Jarman (nee Bennett)

Aunt Phoebe Bennett
Born: 4th December 1805
Died: 8th August 1884
Married John Jarman as his second wife

When widowed she lived at Skellorn Green, Adlington. Her cottage was very small with "one room up, one down" without stairs. Access to the bedroom was by ladder and trapdoor. The bedroom just contained her bed and a chest with initials I.B. At the side of the cottage was a small lean-to shed from which she sold sweets. These were weighed on a simple hand held balance. Martha Ann Wright visited her as a young girl.

Phoebe's niece, Mary Bennett, was her executor whose account book shows that these memorial cards cost 6 shillings.

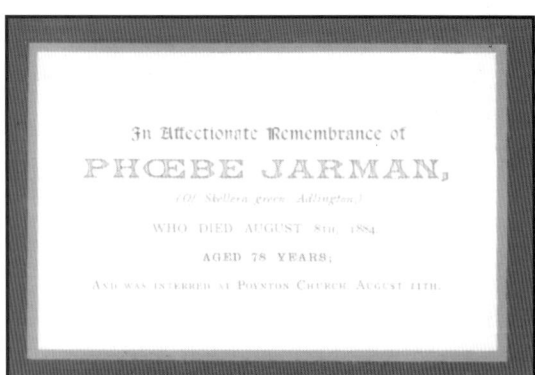

Aunt Phoebe Jarman (nee Bennett) made a simple will, bequeathing her furniture and goods to her late husband John Jarman's children, her nieces and nephews. One of her nieces, Mary Bennett, was her executor.

Mary Bennett's account book records the funeral and executor's expenses. In 1884 a simple funeral cost £4-0s-6d for an elm coffin, a hearse, and men wearing "mourners fittings".

Relatives received memorial cards which cost 6 shillings. Church dues cost 14 shillings. The funeral meal consisted of beef, peas, potatoes and cucumber followed by currant bread and cakes. Wine and brandy were served. Total cost, £1-8s-7d.

These pages show the beneficiaries signatures, signed over stamps, who each received £5-2s-0d.

Mary Bennett 1835 - 1905

Two photographs by Fenley, Ardwick Green, Manchester
Mary Bennett is wearing lace collar and cuffs over her black mourning dress, c. 1883. The left-hand picture shows details of the dress skirt. Close up details of her hand made
lace collar and cuffs are shown in chapter 3.

Two photographic proofs show another dress style with lace collar bow and cuffs.

2

Family Recipes

Our inherited large collection of Martha Ann Wright's family letters and papers revealed a vellum envelope containing two fragile cookery books and many handwritten recipes. These have been scripted for easier reading and a small selection is included here.

Written among the food recipes are home care remedies for common complaints and others for household cleaning and stain removal. These have been grouped together separately. This knowledge was essential first aid for families and lady's maids. Doctors charged patients for all their services, sending a bill at the end of a course of treatment, so they were only used in more serious conditions.

Some recipes are dated and named, the earliest one is for Spung Cake, dated 27th March 1828, Mrs Grubb, The Beach. An envelope gives the whole address of Mrs Harrington, The Polygon, Ardwick, Manchester, then a residential suburb. Mrs T.A.B. Bent, 5 Leaf Square kept a small notebook containing her inventories of linen and silver. At the back of the notebook, in the same handwriting is Rev. and Mrs W.T. Blathewayt's inventory of linen. A separate inventory for servants is written underneath, listing in addition to bed linen and linen towels, table cloths, tea cloths, glass cloths, knife cloths and dusters.

In larger country houses the kitchen was used for cooking only. Food storage was in a store room, food preparation in the larder, dishwashing in the scullery or pantry depending on the type of dishes and the level of dirt. In reality most middle class houses had a multi-purpose kitchen. They employed one servant/cook who often slept in the kitchen.

The kitchen fire place was the heart of the home, so it needed to be well maintained for efficient use. The iron fire grate was cleaned daily and black leaded when cold, in the early morning, about three times a week. The chimney was swept regularly to prevent soot falling into the food.

Once cooking was finished for the day, the servant/cook let the fire die down. When cool enough, the fire embers were 'riddled' to separate ash from cinder. Ash was disposed of, but cinders were reused to lay the fire ready for early the following morning. When burning well, a large container of water would be boiled on the fire and breakfast cooked for the family. Various cooking methods were used depending on the heat of the fire. Recipes mention slow, medium and hot fires, when a joint could be roasted. Sometimes a spit or roasting jack was used to rotate the joint. A fire screen reflected heat back on to the joint which cooked more quickly. It also protected anyone working nearby.

A kitchen range was invented with a side oven and water boiler on either side of the fire, so allowing more cooking to take place at the same time.

Kitchen Fireplaces

The kitchen fire was the main source of heating and cooking. Food was boiled, stewed, fried, roasted, toasted and baked in the oven. Also it was dried and smoked, when hung overhead, to preserve it for winter meals.

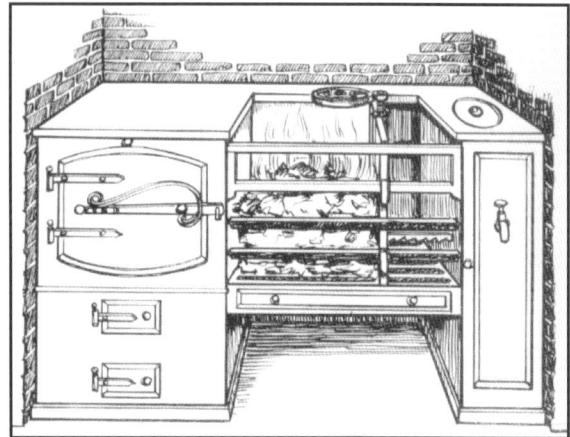

Cast iron kitchen range, providing cooking facilities and a boiler, late 18th century.

Georgian kitchen fireplace with roasting spit and turning pulley. A drip-tray to collect the fat and juices lies on the flagged floor below.

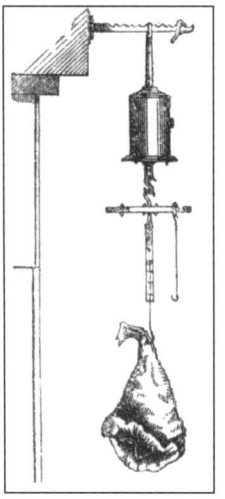

A roasting jack could be hung inside a firescreen for extra, reflected heat.

Celebration meals - table plans

The plans as shown are ¼ scale reconstructions using a modern font.

The original plans were hand-written on opposite sides of a long piece of paper which had been joined in the middle by tacking stitches 9 (approx. size 38" by 8")

Side or corner dishes were known as entrees because they we there when the diners entered the room. The first course, of soup, was placed nearest the entrance. Similar dishes were placed on opposite sides and corners and the head and foot of the table.

Isinglass was used for thickening, instead of cornflour, in sauces or blancmanges.

The meal on the left offers 24 dishes. The larger meal on the right offers 42 dishes, including more meats, lobster, fruit and other puddings.

Left table plan

Pheasant	Soup	Tongue
	Sponge	
	Lebster	
	B. Meng	
Pies	Trifle	Pheasant
	Tart	
Pidgeons		Ham
Chicken	Flowers	Turkey
Pheasant		Pidgeons
	Spenge	
Lebster	Jelly	p.Beef
	Dark B.Menge	
Tongue		Pheasants
	R-Beef	

Right table plan

Pheasant	Soup	Pheasant
Pheasant	Lebster	Miner Pies
Cress Tart	Dark B.Menge	
Chicken Cucumber	Trifle	Tongue Apricots
	Chees Cakes	Pies
	Snow Cheese	
Petted Beef	Sponge	
Pidgeons Apples	Lebster	Pidgeons Oranges
	Flowers	p.Ham
	Lebsters	
Pies Sponge	Sponge	
	B.Menge	
Tongue Apricots	Jelly	Turkey Cherries
	Cheese Cakes	Miner Pies
Cress Tart	Snow Cheese	
	B.Menge	
Pheasant	Lebster	Pheasant
	Beef	

17

To preserve food for the winter months, joints, fish and herbs were hung overhead to be dried and smoked. Some recipes give instructions on how to make marmalade, and how to bottle whole oranges, plums and blackcurrants. Isinglass was used to thicken sauces, blancmange and jelly.

An original long table plan was found among the recipes. There was an accepted way of laying out a table for a celebration meal. Cold dishes were already in place, hot dishes were carried in just before the guests entered the dining room.

Food Recipes

1 To make a Spung (Sponge) Cake

Take the weight of five eggs in lump sugar, the weight of three eggs in fine flour, one lemon. Brake five eggs in a deep pan. Grate the rind of the lemon in the eggs and a little juice. Pound and sift the sugar . Put it in. Get a panning of boiling water. Put the pan with the ingredients in the boiling water until it is quite hot. Work it with a wisk all the time. When it is sufficiently hot take it out and work it until cool enough for the flour then put it in and stir it a few times. Put it in a hot oven. Put a little butter in a saucepan to melt then put in the mould and let it run well in. Then dust it well with lump sugar. Grease a paper and pin it round the outside of the mould. Put in half a teacupful of hot water when you are working it hot. You must have the oven and the mould quite ready before you begin.

The Beach   March 27ᵗʰ 1828   Mrs Grubb

2 To Pickle Herrings

Take equal quantities of vinegar, port wine and water as much as will cover your herrings. After gutting them let them be rubbed with spices namely cayenne pepper, long pepper, a very little mace and cloves pounded together and then lay them in a flat deep dish sufficiently to allow of them being covered well with the mixture. Tie them up close and let them stay an hour in a very slow oven. They are excellent.

3 Chicken Panada

Boil a chicken in a little stock until quite tender. Take the Skin off the Breast & legs. Mince the breast & legs very fine & pound the Minced Meat in a Mortar & put the bones in the liquor the Chicken was boiled in & set them on the Stove to boil whilst the chicken is pounding. Then mix altogether & rub the whole thro' a Sieve. Put it in a Stew pan & Set it on the stove to Make - but it Must Not boil.

4 Lemon Jelly

An Ounce & half of Isinglas disolved in a pint of water, half pound of sugar disolved in a Gill of water, the juice of 6 Oranges and two Lemons. Grate the Rind of the Lemons into the juice. Strain them all separately & put the jelly into your Mold whilst hot

5 Calve's Feet a l'Espagnol

Dip the Calve's feet in Egg & roll them in bread crumbs that have a little Shallot Thyme & parsley Chopped very fine and a little pepper & salt in them. Do them twice Over with the egg & breadcrumbs. Fry them a light brown. Put them round the dish and the Spanish Sauce in the Middle.

6 Spanish Sauce

Slice two large Onions. Put these in a stew pan with a little Vinegar, a quarter of a pint of Sherry, a Small Clove of Garlick, a truffle chopped, Some Ham cut very fine, a few blades of Mace & as much Gravy as is Requisite. Boil all together very Slow for a quarter of an hour & rub it through a Sieve. Squeeze into it a lemon & Season it with pepper & salt. Lady Wood

7 Ginger Biscuits

One oz of grated ginger, 1 lb. of Flour, Six of Butter $^{3}/_{4}$ lb. of Moist Sugar, put these Ingredients together wet them with cold water 'till they make a part of a proper Stifness. Roll them out then cut them any form you like.

8 To Preserve Green Gage Plumbs

Plumbs for this purpose must be of the finest sort and gathered just before they are ripe. Put them into a pan with a layer of vine leaves under them and over them then a layer of plumbs on that and proceed in this manner till your pan is almost full, then fill it with water and set them on a slow fire. When they are hot and the skins begin to rise, take them off. Take off the skins carefully and put them on a sieve as you do them. Then put them into the same water with a layer of leaves as before. Cover them close that no steam can get out and hang them a considerable distance from the fire till they appear green which will require five or six hours. Then take them up carefully and lay them on a hair sieve to drain. Make a good syrup and boil them in it twice a day for two days. Then take them out and put them in a fine clear syrup. Cover and secure them as you do other things of this nature.   S H

9 Ox Cheek Soup

Put half an Ox Cheek into cold water for two hours and a half Clean it well, put it on the fire with 4 quarts of water, 2 or 3 Carrots, Turnips, Celery heads, Onions.& sweet herbs of all kinds tied up together + a few bay leaves a little lemon peel, a few cloves, black pepper and salt. Let the whole simmer for 4-hours then take out the meat cut it into pieces, reserve of the prime pieces what you will want for use at one time. Let the rest simmer on 'till bedtime. Strain off the liquor and put it by to become a jelly. Take what you want of the jelly for use, put to it the nice pieces of the cheek, the juice of half a lemon, a little cayenne pepper $^{1}/_{2}$ a cup of white wine some boiled force meat balls, hard eggs. A cow's heel is a great improvement.

Home Remedies For Common Complaints

1 To make Cold Cream
February 28th 1840

Melt two ounces of white wax with six ounces of oil of almonds over a gentle fire and pour it out into a large bason or marble morter and keep continualy stiring it till it grows cool, then add gradually half a pint of rose water beating or turning the whole briskly together that the water may be perfectly incorporated with the ointment. It should be kept Covered with rose water wich must be Changed every two or three days. This is a most excellent receipt for chapped skins

2 A sure cure for corns
a teaspoonsfull of tar, a teaspoonsfull of brown sugar, a teaspoonsfull of salt petre, mix it all together to a Salve, and aplye it to the corne

3 A Receipt for a Cough
Take

$1/4$ lb of Honey

$1/4$ lb of Conserve of Roses

$1/2$ oz of Elixir of Vitriol (sulphate of metallic elements)

Put the Honey & Conserve of Roses in a pot before the fire till dissolved then mix the Elixir of Vitriol and the rest stirring the whole well together. Take a Teaspoonful of this mixture last thing at Night and first thing in the Morning also 2 or 3 times in the course of the Day.

4 Receipt for Toothache
M. Bennett

A teaspoonful of Flour, a teaspoonful of Black Pepper and a little whiskey made in a paste and put on either Flannel or Linen rag.

5 For Chilblains
Four quarts of soft water 4 oz of Honey 2 oz pearl ashes $1/2$oz of cloves pounded. boil together all the Ingredients 15 or 20 minutes – then fine it through a linen bag

Household Remedies For Stains

1 To take Stain out of Linen
Wet the linen with Spirits of hartshorn and when it is washed the stain will disappear.

2 Ink for Marking Linen
Three oz of Powder of burnt loose beans tied in a linen Cloth and boiled in a Pint of the Juice of Sloes. It makes a writing far superior to any other.

Hand Written Notebooks

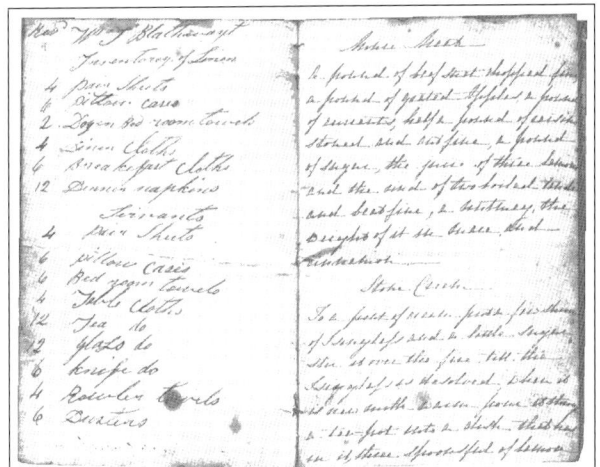

Inventory of the linen for Rev. W.T. Blathwayt and for servants listed below. Serveral recipes follow, the last one for Plum Pudding is signed Ellen Johnson and dated 17th November 1843.

Two inventories belonging to Mrs. T.A.R Bent, No.5 Leaf Square. These are written at the opposite end of the above notebook.

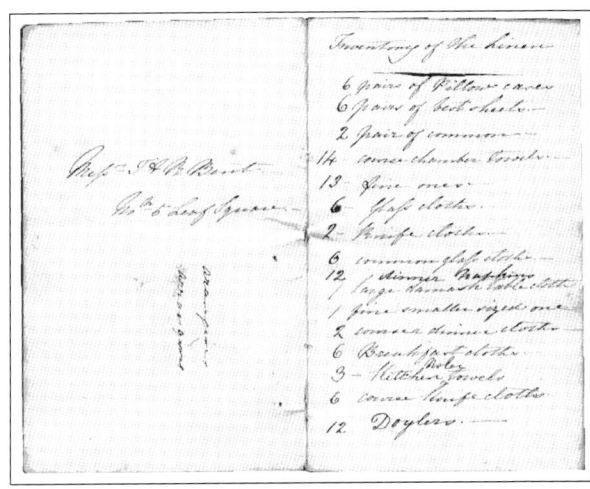

Mrs.Bent's linen

Mrs.Bent's plate

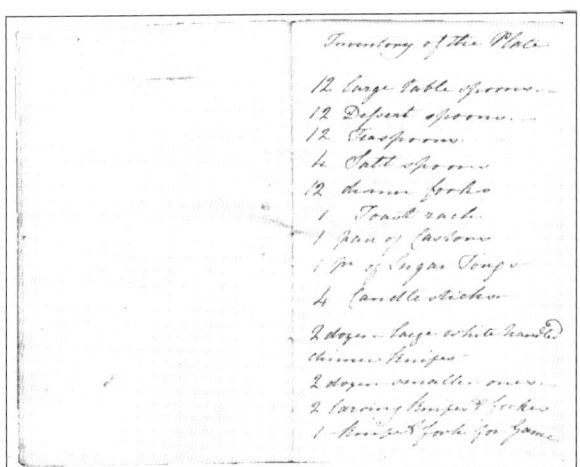

"Linament for rubbing with" Doctor's prescription for Mrs.Bent's servant, dated March 22nd 1885.

3

The Life and Letters of a Lady's Maid

This background information about the life and duties of a Lady's Maid will help to clarify Ann's letters, written to her mother and sister between 1860 and 1864. Letters from servants are extremely rare. A lady's maid was better educated and had a little spare time to write home.

There was often a sense of pride in working at the big house as a servant. Country houses of the 19th century were the largest employers in rural areas, where there were fewer jobs and labour was cheap. Country people were chosen as they were believed to be healthier and stronger to work longer days and were more willing to take orders. In 1871 census, 79% of domestic servants came from rural areas; only 10% of lady's maids were over 40 and they were unmarried. Most female servants hoped to marry before they were 30 years old.

Usually girls did not enter general domestic service until they were 16 or 17 years old. Often they had another job first so that they could earn enough money to buy or make their own uniform usually in black. Sometimes they had to borrow the money from family or friends or pay it back from their small quarterly wages. Three sets of clothes were needed - print dresses for mornings or dirty work, black dress, white cap and apron for afternoons, town clothes for outdoors and church on Sundays. They were always expected to wear a hat and gloves outside and generally to look clean and tidy.

Lady's maids were usually chosen from better-educated girls who had served an apprenticeship in dressmaking, millinery and hairdressing. They were often of a more gentile and polite nature than an ordinary servant and needed to get on with their mistress. In addition to her other duties the lady's maid was expected to know about medical matters, beauty aids and stain removal using just ordinary household materials. As she accompanied her mistress when travelling, she needed to be an experienced luggage packer. She needed to be well dressed at all times as she was always at her lady's beck and call.

Younger women were usually chosen to be lady's maids because they were physically stronger to work long hours each day. They had neat fingers needed for hairdressing, sewing and fastening tiny hooks and buttons, often at the back of clothing. So her mistress was entirely dependent on help in getting dressed and undressed at any time of day or night.

A Victorian lady's dress consisted of layers of warm clothing and skirts made with yards of material. There was a permanent fear that a chill would lead to a cold and complications. Fashionable women wore crinoline frames underneath their layers of petticoats and skirt weighing about 37 lbs, in contrast to today's modern lightweight clothing weighing just over 2 lbs. When wet the clothing became saturated, greatly increasing its weight. So the Victorian lady stayed indoors when it rained. If she was caught in a sudden shower an umbrella only protected her head and she needed to find shelter as shown in the letters from Llandudno.

The lady's maid generally made her lady's clothing and often altered or designed it. New material and trimmings were chosen by the lady for a garment. The new dress was kept for best. All her other dresses were downgraded for visiting or morning wear. If a garment was out of fashion it would be given to the lady's maid, who would then remake it to fit and suit herself. Ann made a small needle case from a scrap of olive green silk left over from her dressmaking. The lady's maid carried her most used tools on a chatelaine belt around her waist. The needle case and chatelaine are shown in the colour plates.

The lady's maid's day began early. In the morning she wakened her mistress with tea, toast or plain biscuit, and open the bedroom curtains. Her mistress discussed plans for the day and which clothes she would be wearing. The maid would pour out a large jug of hot water, carried up from the kitchen, into a china bowl. She would then lay out her mistress' clothes, including underwear, help attend to her toiletries, help her dress and arrange her hair. Later, the maid would wash and starch any clothing, dry and iron it, using flat irons heated on the fire. She might have to repair garments and trim her lady's bonnet. When fine, if her mistress wished to go out for a walk, the lady's maid would be summoned upstairs to help her mistress to change her clothing. If the family were entertaining or attending a function, the lady's maid had to wait up for her mistress to come home after the dinner, often very late. Then she would undress her, help her into aired nightclothes, plait her hair and help her into bed. A cotton nightcap held her hair in place, which replaced the lace cap worn during the day. Then the maid would attend to her clothing, removing any stains before hanging it up. She would put out any washing to be done the following morning before going to bed for a few hours sleep. The lady's maid was given special privileges like her own room, which was cleaned for her by the other servants

In the servants' 'pecking order', the lady's maid held the same status as the butler and housekeeper. Only these three servants were summoned upstairs to the family. Trust developed between the lady and her maid who became her confidante. A friendship developed with her mistress' family and if she left there was a feeling of rejection. The other servants suspected that her loyalty lay with the family and not with them. If the lady's maid gossiped about the family, she faced instant dismissal, without a reference. The lady's maid often felt isolated, as she was not fully accepted by the family nor the other servants.
The lady's maid would expect to earn about £30 a year, in addition to her accommodation. Often she could save a small "nest egg" which was an attraction to a young man wishing to marry and set up home. Together with her many skills, she made a good wife and mother.

Manuals like "The Complete Servant" by Samuel and Sarah Adams, published in 1825, describe the duties of a lady's maid –

"The lady's maid generally has to be near the person of her lady properly qualified for the situation, her education superior to an ordinary female servant, particularly in needlework and useful and ornamental branches of female acquirements. To be perculiarly neat and clean in her person is better than to be tawdry or attractive:- as intrinsic merit is a greater recommendation than extrinsic appearance. In temper, cheerful and submissive, studying her lady's disposition and conforming to it with acrility as a soft and courteous demeanour will best entitle her to esteem and respect. Her character should be remarkable for industry and moderation. Her manners and deportment for modesty and humility. Her dress for neatness, simplicity and frugality".

Letters from Lady's Maid Ann Bennett

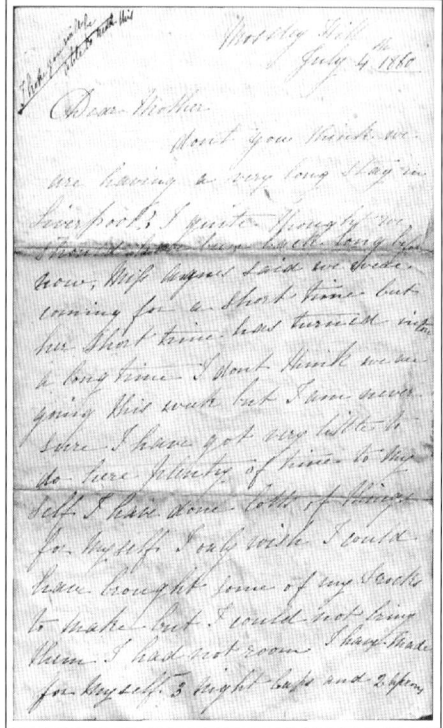

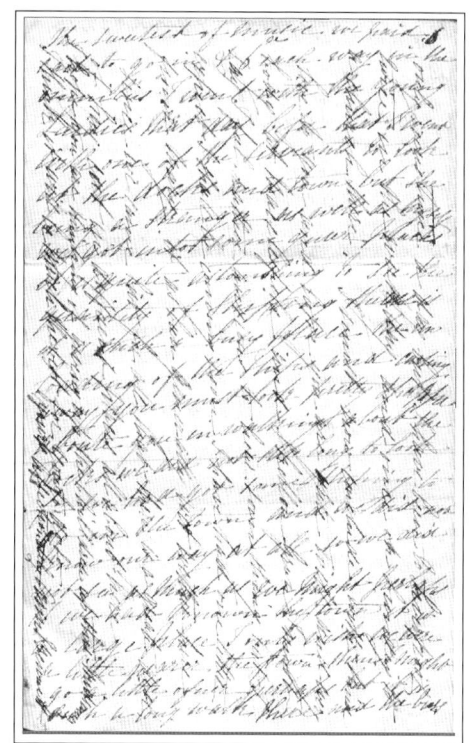

Ann has written across her last page as notepaper was expensive at the time.
Her letters have been scripted for easier reading.

Envelope addressed to Mary Bennett, servant for Miss Priestnall.

Ann Bennett

Ann Bennett

Lady's Maid to Miss Agnes Greg at the Mount

Alfred Wright
Joiner at LowerHouse Mill and to the
Gregs at the Mount, married Ann Bennett
at Prestbury Church 22nd December 1864.

Mary Bennett, elder sister to Ann

Sunday February 12th 1860

Dear Sister,

I am writing to you according to promise but have sad news to tell you. My Uncle George Died yesterday Morning betwixt 10 and 11 o'clock. My Aunt Betty came from here about 3 o'clock to let us know he was dead and we were quite astonished because he appeared so much better on the Friday Night when My Father was there, so we all thought he would continue for a while but he went so sudden at the last. Mr Cawley had been down to see him in the Morning and pray for him and when he was gone by Aunt Betty thought that she would go up stairs and see how he was and when she got up stairs ---he had raised himself up and sat on the bedside, so she called My Aunt Grace up and they Got him into bed again. My Aunt Grace said he was dying and My Aunt Betty went at once for Mr Cawley. She and he came down then he died almost directly.

My Father has been up every night in the week. One night he stayed altogether so that my Aunt Sarah Might go to bed for she was almost wearied out and they thought they had better send for My Aunt Grace. So she came on Friday Night and very well it was as it so happened. His las(t) complaint was an inflamation in his side. My Father fetched Mr Schofield last Tuesday Night, so he came on Wednesday Morning and he thought he was improving on the Friday when he was there but it seems not long for this life. Every body seems so shocked when they hear of his death. He has gone so soon but we hope he is better off.

They have arrainged for him to be buried on Thursday. Do you think you can come? We have not heard any particulars yet. My Father is up there today. I most likely should have gone two, but I have been so poorly all day and not fit to go out. My Mother and I thought to have gone this afternoon but we were both a great deal to poorly to go out at all.

I came home from the Mount on Thursday Night I have not been up to Skellorn Green so I have not seen him and I feel very sorry They came from (Hazel) Grove on Friday to see him My Aunt Pheby came today and was quite struck when she heard.

I expect to hear more when my Father comes home I expect to be busy this week before the Funeral and after two. I have begged off from Mrs Clayford or else I ought to have been there this week.

Good Night

From your affectionate

Sister Ann Bennett

Mossley Hill
July 4th 1860

I hope you will be able to read this

Dear Mother

Don't you think we are having a very long stay in Liverpool? I quite thought we should have been back long before now. Miss Agnes said we were coming for a short time but her short time has turned into a long time. I don't think we are going this week but I am never sure. I have got very little to do here plenty of time to myself. I have done lots of things for myself. I only wish I could have brought some of my frocks to make but I could not bring them I had not room. I have made for myself 3 night caps and 2 aprons a white Petticoate beside working a collar and some other little things. I have made 2 Night Gowns for Miss Boundalls and lots of little things for Miss Agnes that don't take up much time. It was quite laughable to night to see the 2 old ladies go off tonight dresst for a dinner party with their hoods on over their Caps. Miss Agnes as been rather gay since she has been here. She has been to several dinner parties in full dress. Miss Sally came home last week from Malvern and Mrs Reynolds was to have gone tomorrow to New Brighton but they are disappointed in their lodgings so they are not going at present. I heard Miss Agnes say she should like very much to go to Bangor and Miss Sally said I will go with you any time, so I think it very likely she will be going there soon but I have not other foundations for saying so. It may possible blow over as some things do.

I heard a wisper that we were going to have a change in Bollington soon. Emma is leaving and going to Norcliff to live but don't name a word to anyone. Miss Agnes is looking out for me. I think there will be one engaged. she has not named a word to me.

Miss Agnes treated me the other day to St Georges Hall to hear the Grand Organ played. I suppose it is one of the largest organs in the world. It was played one hour. I think I never heard anything so Grand. It is in a fine Spacious room and seemed altogether like thunder and sometimes so faint you might have thought it the sweetest music. We paid 6d each to go in and 6d each way in the omnibus. I went with the Young Ladies that day. Before that I went with one of the servants to look at the docks and town but she being a stranger as well as myself we got into some queer places. It is quite astonishing to see the quayside of Shipping Hulls is it is thick and busy place. The unloading of the ships and casting away you must look pretty sharp about you in walking about the Docks. We did not stop long to look for had got some shopping to do in the town and we did not know our way at all for we did not see as much as we might perhaps, if we had known the town. It is a large place I only wish we were a little nearer the town then I might go a little ofner perhaps but is is much too long a walk there and the bus only runs twice a day. But I have been to Liverpool twice in the weekday and once on Sunday to a church there I must now conclude with x and love to you and hope you are quite well and everybody at Macclesfield and Skellorn Green. I must say I feel rather anxious to hear something but I expect I shall be coming soon. I have had one letter from Mary. It has been generally wet weather here since we came but for all that there is a great deal of hay out in different places all about here. I hope you are thinking of giving up the Chilldren up this Midsummer. I think it will be much the best for you.

Yours affectionately

Ann Bennett   _____

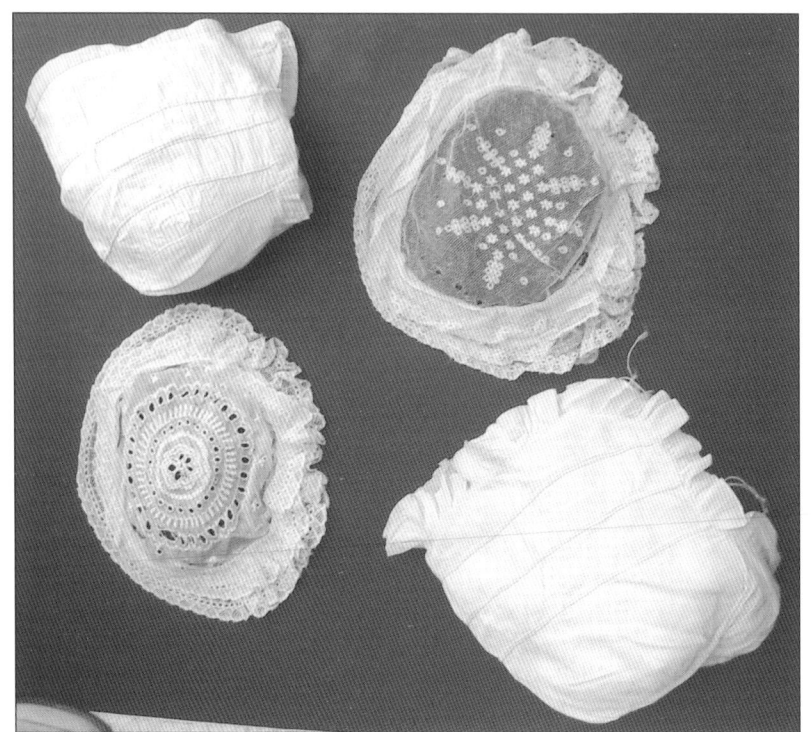

Lace caps were worn
by day and cotton night
caps at night.
These were handmade
by Ann Bennett

Mary Bennett's lace collar and
cuffs shown on her dress in
chapter 1

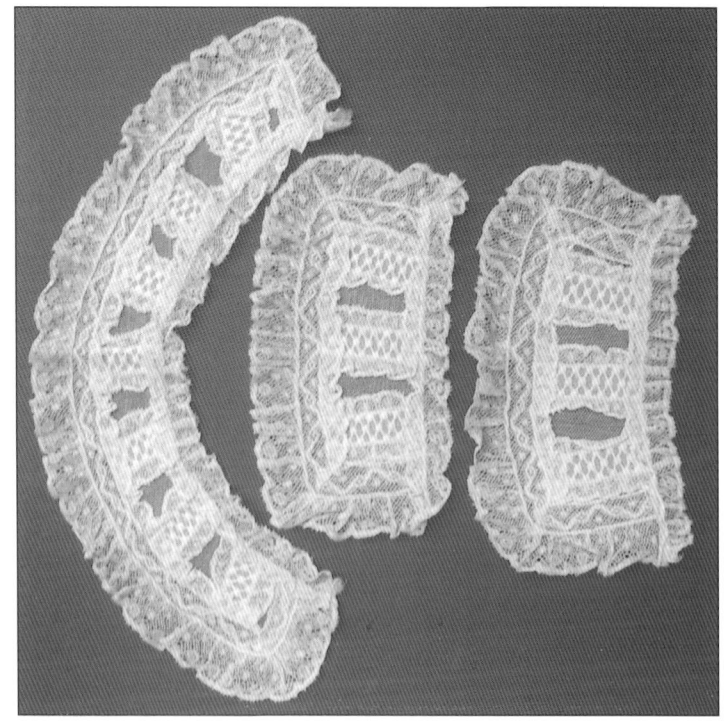

9 St Georges Terrace Llandudno.
July 16 1861

My dear Sister

I received your kind letter and am happy to tell you that I am enjoying myself as well as I am, considering I am a stranger in a strange place. I have made several adventures on the Mountains. The first time I went on Great Orme's Head. I and one of the servants that is staying in this house went together one night both of us perfect strangers and the consequence was we were lost on the top of the mountain. There was not a creature to be seen as it was getting quite dusk and there we were chasing about for our very lives trying to find a track down fearing we might stay there all night amongst the sheep and goats. We could see the houses and the sea but could not get down amongst the rocks. At last we did find a beaten track and almost came down head first. We were so glad. We got in the house about ten o'clock and fully made up our minds not to go so far on the mountains so late at night.
The first time we went upon Little Orme's Head it came on a heavy shower. When we were on the top so of course the grass became very slippery and in coming down I got such a jolly fall on my back. You would have laughed to have seen me with my umbrella flying away but I feel the affects of my fall yet, particularly in going up and down stairs. I had a bathe in the sea yesterday morning for the first time. it was the finest day we have had since we came. I should have liked very much to have gone in the steamer to Bangor and Carnarvon but I do hope to go before I leave here. It is such a pity to miss the bridges when we are so near them. I have had a letter from home this morning and my mother tells me my Uncle John and Aunt Betty (Underhill) are coming to Rhyl and very likely may come down here and call upon me. I should very much like them to come because the scenery is so beautiful. They have had an accident at Hope Green perhaps you have heard of it. It is very sad to think off. She tells me they are very busy in the garden. I shall miss the finish this season and I am afraid Father and Mother are pretty well, only tired with there work.

The end of the letter is missing

---

9 St Georges Terrace
July 16 1861

Dear Mother

I was very pleased to receive a letter from you and I would say I am enjoying myself as much as I can considering I am a stranger in a strange place. I have made two or three adventures on the mountains I and another went one night on Great Orme's Head both of us perfect strangers and the consequence was we were lost on the top. We had ascended of one mountain on to another until we were so high and it was getting quite dusk and there we were chasing about for our very lives trying to find a track down again. We began to fear we might not get down again before it was quite dusk. At last we did find a way down and came almost head first. We got in about 10 o'clock and fully made up our minds not to go on the Mountains so late again. My first adventure on Little Orme Head we had daylight on our side but it came on a heavy shower when we were on the top so in coming down I got such a jolly fall on my back my umbrella flew away and away I went. I feel the affects of it yet. I am very stiff particular going up and down stairs. I went down and had a bathe in the sea yesterday morning for the first time. Yesterday was the finest day we have had since we came. I should liked to have gone to Bangor and Canarvon in the steamer but I trust I shall go before I leave I should not like to miss the Bridges when I am so near them.

The houses are thinly scattered, one little place fixed here and there under the sides of the mountains to shelter them from storms. I shall be very glad to see my Uncle and Aunt if they can make it convenient to call and it would be a pity for them to come to Rhyl and not take a trip down here. I am sorry to hear of that accident so near and so hard for people to …… such a way. I hope you will not tizzy yourself so much with the cleaning but never mind doing so much. I hope my Father keeps well. I am afraid I shall lose the fruit altogether this season but it ……..be now.

I have had a letter from Mary. She is very well. I must conclude with kind love to you from your affectionate daughter

Ann Bennett

Mossley Hill
August 4 1862

Dear Sister

You will think me a long time about writing but I heard a wisper about us going to see a Dioramma of Jerusalem and the Holy Land in town. We were to have gone on Saturday then today but Miss A is not very well so it is just off again so I begin to fear it will not be at all I thought I would not write until I had been to see it but it is so long in coming. I have been pretty well since the first day after I came I had the toothache so bad I scarcely knew what to do it lasted so long but I got a little sleep. The next morning it was better and I have not had it since but the soreness has not left me yet. It was so bad I never had it worse. I fully determined to have them drawn if it continued long

I had a pleasant journey here only that I was so tired of waiting at London Road and it is such a horrible place. All about the booking office for the Liverpool line I could scarcely stir. I think they are building a new station what with mortar bricks and timber and workmen and trains it is a most difficult place and the Porters belonging the Liverpool line will not carry the passengers Luggage to the L & N Western side. I just met Mrs Brogend there. She got off the train which I was going by. The Porter would not take her bag across nor yet call another porter to do it. I think I was very fortunate to get my box carried across. When I came the porter was very good. He took my luggage and gave it in charge of the book keeper. He said I could not possible wait there. He took me to the waiting room on the other side the L & N Western side. When I booked for Liverpool I had 2d to pay for my boxes but I did not mind that I came remarkable cheap. The fare was 2s7½d. The train only runs to Garston. Busses take the passengers to Liverpool. They took me too far down. I should have got out at Aigburth and being strange I did not quite know the way. They put (me) down and my boxes in the road to the mercy of anyone but fortunately 2 boys came up with a cart and one said he would take my box to Aigburth post office for 2d. Then I was fast again. I enquired if there was any means of getting to Mossley Hill. The man said no there was none. I did not know what to do. I thought Miss Sally's man would not like fetching it up and I did

The rest of the letter is missing

---

57 Oak Hill Terrace
Hoghton Street
Southport

Dear Sister

I feel very anxious not to hear something from you, but I suppose you are waiting for me to write. I have not much to write about so you must excuse a long letter from me this time. We have been here a week last Wednesday and had pretty tolerable weather. I think Southport rather a pretty place and quite like a town, such wide open streets and quite a nice Market Hall, a great many nice buildings; the town hall and churches and Chapels. Altogether it looks a very fair place. There is a very fine pier goes right away into the sea but is a penny a day or 6 farthing to walk on, so I am content to walk on the promenade for the sea air. The sands are so rough you cannot walk on them. I was down one morning when the tide was up. It was a fine sea and so refreshing. Yesterday and today are so wet there is no getting out. The cabs amuse me as much as anything. They run three donkeys abreast. Of they trot away so fast. They are quite respectable looking cabs. More of them run donkeys than horses a great deal.
 I hear we are going to have a change at the Mount. Mrs Gregs Cook is leaving so Catherine is going into the best kitchen and we must have a fresh one again. We have constant changes at our side but is it what we may expect
We came here for 3 weeks so I hope you will not be long before you write to me and send me all the news you can. I have written home but have not heard anything yet, so perhaps you will not be long before you write to me so with kind love

I wish you Good Bye

From your loving sister
Ann Bennett

Don't forget to send me all instructions about the Bradley and all you can think about. Miss A is not down yet 12 o'clock. She wont be long I should hope now. Next time I hope to have more to write about.
57 Oak Hill Terrace Hoghton Street Southport

Escowbeck, - Caton
August 13th 1863

My Dear Mother

You see we are really come at last and it is truly a pretty place. We had a very comfortable journey except for the dust in some parts of the way. It was an Express train and a tremendous length from Newton junction for the North. The Shooting Season commenced yesterday so a Gentleman told us. There were not so many passengers as there had been the previous two days, so I think it must have been terrible then. We were well powdered all over and nearly choked with the dust. I suppose owing to the length and speed of the train. The carriage and Pair met us at Lancaster so I came outside with the coachman and had a view of the country as we came along. I have not been out yet so cannot tell much of the place, but there is a beautiful park and lodge and there seem nice walks and a pond in front with boats so nice I think. It is a very nice house but I have not been in any of the lower rooms yet (but) there is a fine staircase with such handsome large pictures hanging on the walls. I do feel so strange and lost, yet the servants all except one strangers to me, but I will try and get out and see all I can. I must try and see the castle and get down to the town, only it is 4 miles off but shall feel more at home bye and bye and can ask more questions about things and shall be able to tell you more next time I write if I do write again.

But we are only staying a week or 11 days at the very outside. I expect Mrs Milly is coming here tomorrow so I shall have her to wait upon, which will give me a little more to do. I have not much now. Miss Sally and the babe are still at Bollington and will be there I expect when we return. Sarah and Mrs B did not half like Miss A going away and taking me and leaving them with company but I think Miss A will get home as soon as she possible can. We shall have the wedding before long so she will be at home again soon. You may give Mary this letter and I shall be glad to hear something if she has time to write to me. I wonder how she is getting on with Mrs C, wether she thinks she can manage the work. I thought she might perhaps be at Prestbury on Sunday Morning, but she was not there.

Miss Agnes has just gone out for a walk in the garden the day is turned out beautiful. I think I must get out too this afternoon or evening for a walk.

How is your arm going on and how is my Father now? I have not heard any more about the house at present but I don't see why it should not answer for you very well if the rent is moderate. That is the main thing. I don't think off anything more now.

So Good bye with love

Your Affectionate daughter

Ann Bennett

Mr John Greg Esquire is the Mayor of Lancaster
Now Mr John Greg Esquire
Escowbeck
Caton Nr Lancaster

Ann's letter was posted in this envelope posted Lancaster 13 August 1863.
It was also postmarked Macclesfield 14 August 1863 on the reverse.

Mossley Hill Mrs Reynolds
Wavertree
Nr Liverpool

Mossley Hill June 7 1864

My dear Sister

I arrived here on Saturday Afternoon after 4 o'clock I had a very comfortable journey except for the long wait of more than 2 hours at London Road Station.
Alfred came to the station at Prestbury to see me off so I got plenty of attention. One man to put me in the carriage and another man to put my luggage in. I heard from Alfred this morning he said such an intolerable dejection of spirit crept over him after I left him and remained with him all day he could not cast it off he told me.

Sarahs front gave satisfaction. I hope the interview was successful on Sunday. When you write tell me all about it. We are staying here about a fortnight and then going home. I have not lost much time since I came on Sunday I and Agnes went to Mrs Williams to tea and met her two brothers and her sweetheart. He came in on Saturday and will be away again tomorrow. I don't know when Sam will be going out with his vessel. He was particularly attentive to me. He walked home with me on Sunday night and yesterday there was a party of us went a Pic Nic to Eastham so I went with Sam. He payed all my expences I scarcely liked him to pay for me but he did and behaved like a Gentleman he did not take the slightest liberty any more than if I had been a married woman ever so and still payed me the greatest possible attention he was so proper in every thing he is really a nice young man – somebody teased him and said it was not to late to set another young man by but he made answer and said he would never have an action of that sort to answer for. It was not in my presence it was said. He came all the way home with me last night. It was after 11 o'clock when we got home but he never said much about Alfred only asked me what he did, so I told him and said he was not loose yet but that he was very quiet and steady. So he told me I was not too old to wait a while and that was worth waiting for. He talked so sensible to me. We had a splendid day for crossing the water and we enjoyed ourselves immensely every one of us so much so that I feel the effects rather to much today. I am so stiff I can scarcely move but I will tell you all particulars when I come back. Mr Johnson was there and I never met with a more jocular man in my life. He is just the man to amuse a party like that. He kept us laughing all the time such fun he made in every way. I cannot pretend to write it all, only one thing I got my frock dirty from end to side with you know what sort of dirt and he very decently cleaned me. That was one of my messes he declared. His hands smelled of sugar as he called it when he was coming home. He really is a most amusing man. I am sure you will laugh when I tell you the events of the day throughout when I come back. I can scarcely walk today with my running and walking yesterday I can hardly stir my legs.

I don't think I shall write home yet so you may tell my mother all you can out of this letter. Tell her I saw her looking out of the garden but the compartment was full so I could not get near the window to shew myself.

Alfred told me he went over on Saturday but he did not give me particulars so I hope you will when you write.

What a very laughable affair happened at Adlington station on Sunday morning. No doubt you will have heard all particulars about such like things don't happen very often nowadays. It will long be remembered but not a very pleasant remembrance to the parties concerned in it. My arm and hand both ache with writing so I think it is about time I gave up.

I have written two long letters now one to Alfred also so I have done pretty well at one spell so with much love to Sarah and you I remain

Your Affectionate Sister

Ann Bennett

Agnes said Good Bye to her Robert last night for 5 weeks at the least what a parting and meeting there must be one thinks. I wonder what Alfred would do but I suppose they get used to it like everything else. Good Bye A.B.

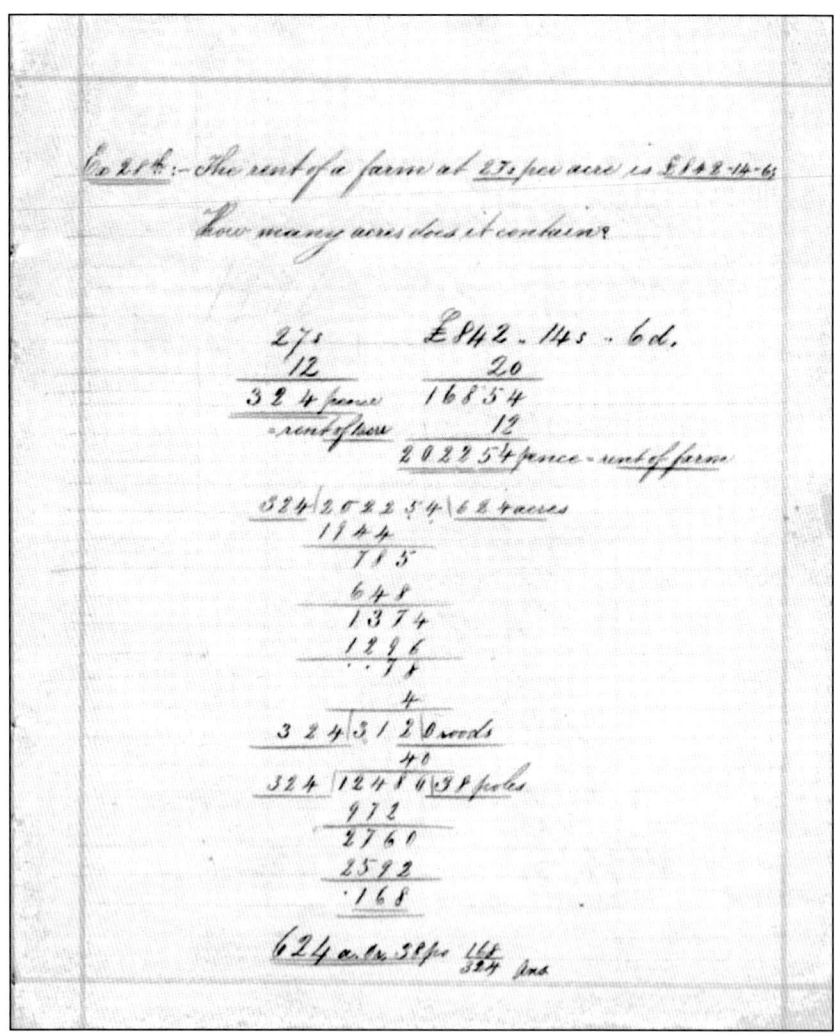

A page from Alfred Wright's Arithmetic Copybook.

The Mount
October 31 1864

My Dear Mother

I dare say you are out of all common patience with Alfred as he does not come and finish his work there. I have asked him often to come and he thought himself he would come last Saturday and previous Saturday also but some how it as both times slipped through. He has been busy with one thing or other all the time. His father has come here to live and he of course wanted his help all he could in fixing up and making things a little different. Last Saturday he was putting a table up in the shop for him. I don't think he will come next Saturday either. Him and I quite purposed coming over last Sunday but I could not come there were so many in the house and Faith is still away so I have to help to wait dinner on a Sunday when there are too many for one and there were 18 of them, but if next Sunday is fine and I can get away we will come then and I hope Alfred will really come the following Saturday. He has been so busy too preparing things for himself. Poor lad! I don't know how he manages to think of everything he had bought pans and jellies and baking tins and tea caddy and tray and spice box and lamps and candlesticks and fire irons and flat irons and tin mugs and fenders and fire bellows, which I told him we might have done without, and stair rods and carpeting and coconut matting for our room and a clock. He wants me to make a hearthrug of some bits of cloth but I don't know how to begin that job but I must try I suppose to please him as he wants one. He says he thinks we must have a house with a parlour but he cannot furnish a parlour before Christmas so it must be shut up until such times as we can get furniture for it that is what he thinks now but he may change his mind before then. He is living with his father and boarding at 8/- per week but his money goes as it comes.

When I saw you last I expected he was going to work in Macclesfield. He did go on the Monday morning but was back by dinner time at work in Bollington. He did not like his job so left it at once. He said he would not have stopped at any wage it was such a dirty job. He has been working in Bollington since for Hampson at Olivers Mill. I don't know how long for but really I think it is no use his attempting to leave here for directly he leaves he finds himself back again.

Now I have some more news for you Miss Sally is coming here to live at the Barley Mow. It is being made into a nice house for her. She will bring William from Liverpool and his horse and carriage. She is nearly constantly here. She is going away tomorrow for a few days. She has been here a fortnight and in bed most of the time with a cold so I have been rather busy because Miss A generally gives a meal a day while Faith is away to relieve the other servants a little. I have had a very heavy cold too and sore throat and do feel very low spirited. I fancy they wont be sorry when I come to go and I don't care how soon. I have been quite long enough and a change will suit both them and me. There is a servant engaged for my place with unacceptionable character, 26 years of age. I expect almost all the uncomfortableness arises from myself feeling so dissatisfied. I wish I could feel happier about things and then they would go off easier but instead of that I grumble and then one thing leads to another. However now I have settled in my mind I will be easy while I stay as it is not long now 5 weeks. I wish I was not so miserable but happier in my mind.

Now about my things. I have a great many and I think my best plan will be to get them away as soon as I can. I think I will see the carrier and get him to bring them. I think I will bring them all away with me and then they will be done with but I hope you or someone will be coming over for I never see anyone nor hear anything and I am fast in the house as I don't intend asking to go anywhere if I can help it now. I have some rags and feathers I should like to have away of I could get them anyhow but I am so fast now when I ought to be the most at liberty but so it is. Miss Agnes has never mentioned my leaving and only one day she asked me if I should live in Bollington and gave me 2 oil pictures to frame but only consider one of them worth framing. I have given them to Alfred to do as he likes best with them. I have not got much sewing done. I have cut out my dress and now I have cut the sleeve. I don't like it so well but I think it must do now. I does not much matter as I know off.

Now I think I must conclude with love to you hoping to hear sometimes in some shape or form before long. It is just 10 o'clock and I am sleepy so good night

Your affectionate daughter
Ann

I could say much more but I think I must stop in the hope of slipping over next Sunday if fine.

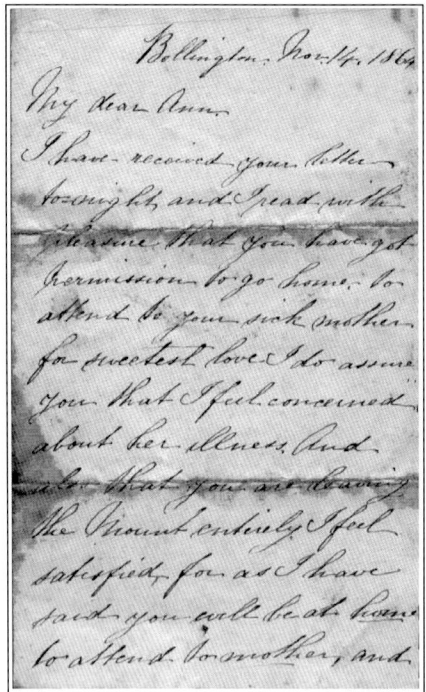 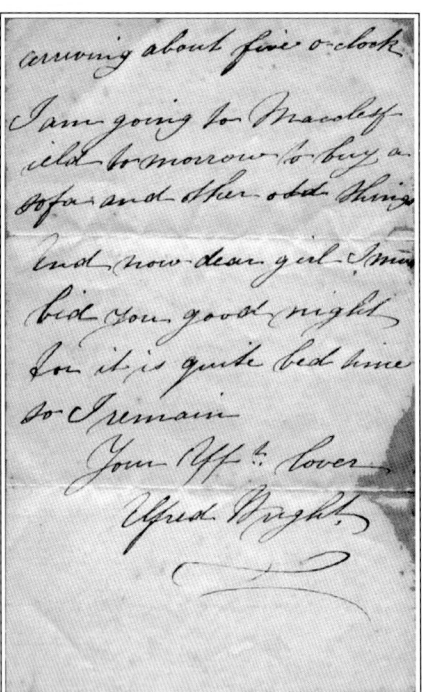

Alfred Wright's letter dated November 14 1864, written to Ann Bennett, his bride-to-be. Ann had taken early leave from her position as Lady's Maid at the Mount to take care of her sick mother at home.

Adelaide Street
Southport July 27 '66

My Dear Sister,

We had a very pleasant journey here except for the long wait in Manchester which was rather tedious but fortunately Charles was so taken up with the Engines moving about that he never cryed at all he had a short sleep in the train from Manchester to Southport be never cried all the way at all. We were a long time before we got lodgings we were running about an hour or two but Mrs Barton was very kind when we found her out. She made us tea and was very kind to us but they were quite full and could not take us in. They sent us to different houses but nobody was just ready to have us then either they were expecting someone or the people were not going for a day or two some were too high. These lodgings which we have are very expensive 30/- per week for 3 bed rooms and a parlour but it is no use we must pay at these places. It is a nice house and very clean so we cannot have every thing. We went to meet Uncle John and Aunt Betty this afternoon but they are not come and we met with Miss Pounall at the station so she is come to tea with us and I cannot so well write with the talking going on so you must excuse much now. I well tell you more next time. Charles has behaved very well so far but we have not been on the sands yet. It was so wet this morning and this afternoon we went to the station and bought a poe for Charles. We went out for meat and potatoes this morning and that was all. We shall go on the sands this evening but I must just scribble over another letter to Bollington.

Now Good Bye for the Present
Your affectionate Sister

Ann Wright (nee Bennett)

Address Mrs Fields Dresden Villas Adelaide Street Southport

Ann had taken baby Charles, born 19 November 1865 to Southport for a week's holiday

Ann Bennett received this Valentine Card and poem, dated Thursday 20 January 1853, from James Clayton Fletcher, Poynton Village, Nr. Stockport

The lacy Valentine card, the greeting reads:- 'Wanted an Affectionate Mate'

Daguerreotype of Ann Bennett about 1853

Family Needlework Tools

Sewing box c. 1790. Mahogany inlaid
with rosewood.

Cotton Reel Stand

Sewing box showing drawer and
contents

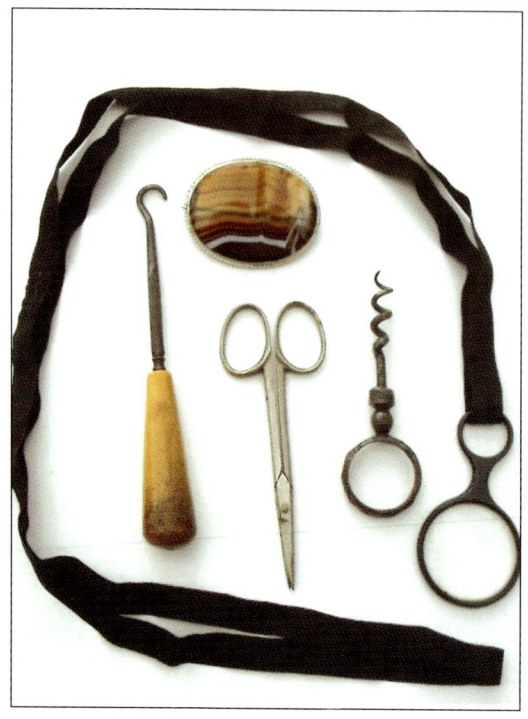

Typical items that hung from a chatelaine, including button hook, scissors cork screw, tortoiseshell brooch and magnifying glass.

Fastenings in jet, metal, black ribbon and braid.

Needle case made by Ann Bennett with original needles and fine stitching.
Actual size 1³/₄" x 1¹/₂"

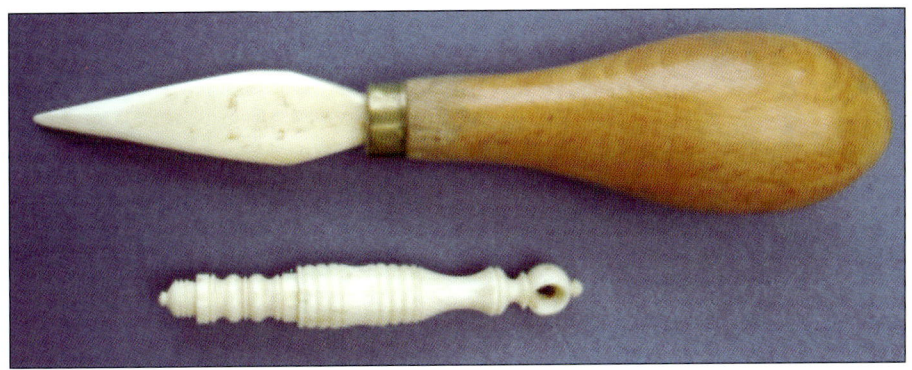

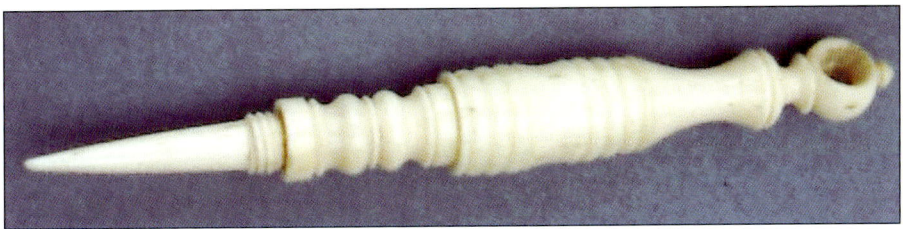

Ivory Stilettos made holes for eyelet embroidery.
The smaller one is shown closed and open

Netting Gauges and needles, one threaded, were used to make coarse
and fine nets which could be embroidered

Berlin Work Patterns

Berlin wool-work patterns which were given free with
"The Young Ladies Journal" of 1866 and 1867

Butterfly Slipper Pattern

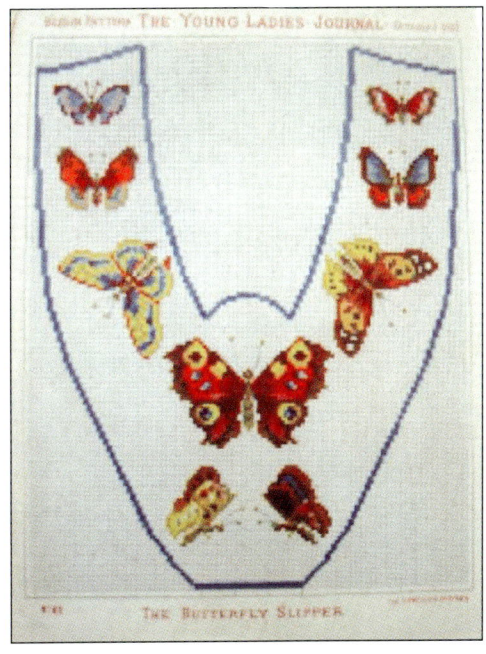

Ann Wright (nee Bennett) had begun to make a butterfly slipper from this pattern from "The Young Ladies Journal" 1 October 1867.

Counted thread work on plain canvas tent stitch with wool. Canvas edges were tacked to prevent fraying. The work was centred by lines of tacking thread shown.

Ann's embroidery sampler motifs worked on linen, raw edges hemmed. Counted thread work in cross stitch using silk threads.
18 inches by 16 inches

Home made Gifts

Manufactured punched card bookmarks and needlecase
were bought and hand-embroidered for small gifts.

Embroidered Postcards fromWorld War I

Alfred Hedley Wright sent these embroidered postcards from France to his cousin Mary and family in Bollington during the First World War

4

Samuel Greg Junior: 1804 - 1876 and Lowerhouse, Bollington

Samuel Greg Junior was born in King Street, Manchester on 6 September 1804. He was the 11th child of 13, born to parents Samuel Greg and Hannah (nee Lightbody) of Quarry Bank Mill, Styal. He was a shy and timid child.

Together with his brothers, he was educated at Unitarian Schools at Bristol and Nottingham, before going to Edinburgh University. During these early years, they all learnt about the family business, before entering the family firm. They were also given the opportunity to travel as representatives of Samuel Greg & Company, meeting customers and sightseeing, which widened their horizons and broadened their business experience.

Samuel Junior entered the family business in 1827 at Quarry Bank Mill, Styal, the 3rd of 4 brothers to do so. An experienced manager supervised their apprenticeships, before they each took over one of the mills in the family group. The older two brothers, Robert Hyde and John, were competent businessmen. Of the younger two brothers, William did not have the temperament. Samuel Junior was an idealist who viewed his business as a social experiment, primarily, rather than a profit making business, to ensure the job security of his workers.

For many years, while at Styal, Samuel Junior and William Rathbone were concerned about the plight of the working classes. They both believed that the appalling conditions of the manufacturing towns led some people into vice and drunkenness. There was a great contrast between the village community conditions provided for the Styal workforce.

A 'To Be Let' notice in the Macclesfield Courier of 1830 gave details of Lowerhouse Mill Bollington which is précised below.

> *Sited on the River Dean it had an extensive reservoir and an iron water wheel of 40 horses power. The Mill was 4 storeys high and an attic, heated by steam. It was equipped for spinning and power loom weaving. Stone built accommodation provided for a mill owner in a dwelling house with garden stocked with fruit trees and 100 acres of meadow and pasture land. Nearby there were 50 workers cottages and a Managers house. Situated in a populous area 2 miles from Macclesfield, 17 miles from Manchester, 1 mile from Manchester to London Turnpike Road, and ½ mile from Macclesfield Canal. Coal mining nearby.*

In 1832 Samuel Greg Junior, a bachelor aged 28 years, moved to Turner Heath, Bollington to take over Lowerhouse Mill. He leased it from the executors of Messrs. Antrobus, from 1832 until 1846, when it was bought by the Gregs. Samuel and his brothers found that the mill was originally built for silk spinning and was powered by a worn out water wheel and a Boulton and Watt steam engine. The mill was an empty shell and during the first two years it needed a lot of work to adapt it for cotton.

Moss Brow cottages and Lowerhouse Mill

Moss Farm with Lowerhouse Mill behind

Lowerhouse Mill and Long Row cottages

Lowerhouse School

There had been a Sunday School at Lowerhouse before 1830, led by two daughters of the mill owner, Philip Antrobus. Deeds show that the building was bequeathed to the Greg family in 1832 on the death of Philip Antrobus. In 1834, Greg writes that the workers had started a Sunday School. The school land and building shown on the Tithe Map and Award 1848 was owned by Samuel Greg. On Sunday afternoons from 1837 or 8, the Wesleyan Methodists held services there, with average congregations of 25 and the building had 250 'free places'. (Ecclesiastical Census 10 March 1851 for Golden Hall (sic) School, signed by John Hayes, steward). There was a Day School for children who were mostly non-conformist. The large hall was used for evening classes, meetings, social functions and the 'Annual Dinnering' for the mill workers and owners. There was also a reading room and library, whose books were stamped 'Goldenthal Library'.

In 1907 Cheshire County Council stopped funding education at Lowerhouse School. The 40 pupils were transferred to Bollington Cross Church of England School. When Greg gave up Lowerhouse Mill in 1906, the mill manager took over the school building, making slight alterations. It continued to be used as a Sunday School and Reading Room.

In 1921, a local builder bought the single story school building and land. He converted it into two separate houses, putting a first floor and dormer windows into the roof space. Painters' graffiti initialled and dated 1923 are in the original dark green paint of the dormer window frames found by one householder during renovation. The Fine Cotton Spinner's Association took over the mill. Their visiting apprentices slept in the school hall, as a dormitory. Many broken pieces of inkwells, slate pencils, writing slates, glass buttons have been found in the garden. Also pieces of broken pottery, one marked *"Lowerhouse Sunday School, Bollington"* around an oval belt motif and a small brass book plate inscribed *"Lowerhouse Sunday School, Bollington 1866"*.

Greg wrote that he found

> *"about 50 cottages, some of them well built and good size, but in extremely bad repair and wanting many little accommodations such as water, coalsheds, cupboards, etc. which are so essential to cleanliness and comfort".*

Samuel first concentrated on the mill building, making reservoirs, putting in shafting and machinery and preparing gas works. Samuel took three fields between the cottages and the mill, divided them up into 6 rood strips for gardens each separated by a neat thorn hedge. The cottages were modernised and the small school building extended.

In 1834, after updating the buildings, he recruited a workforce, some came from Quarry Bank, Styal, to give him a nucleus of experienced workers. Samuel saw his opportunity to influence the lot of his workforce, believing that by providing them with fair wages, comfortable houses, gardens for their vegetables and flowers, schools and other means of improvement for their children, sundry little accommodations in the mill, visiting them when sick or in distress, offering guidance on behaviour, he would improve social harmony between employers and workers.

Samuel began to entertain operatives who showed good manners and characters. He established the "Order of the Silver Cross" to which all girls are eligible for outstanding character and manner. In 1835, Samuel Greg wrote to Mr. Leonard Horner, Inspector of Taxes. He explained in detail how in 1834 the work people were interested in forming a Sunday School with drawing, singing and other classes on week evenings, a good library and reading room and evening parties occasionally during the winter and every facility for innocent recreation including a sports and playing field. He says -

> *"I established the order of Silver Cross among the girls, to which all above the age of 17 or 18 are eligible, this ornament being a distinct mark of superiority of character and manner.... It has been a powerful weapon in my hands to refine the minds, tastes and manners of our cotton maidens and through their influence, of softening and humanising the sterner part of our population".*

In the autumn of 1837 he established some warm baths, men and women using it on alternate days, costing one penny for a ticket. Samuel enjoyed hunting and riding horseback to visit his family at Styal and his friends, the Bromley-Davenports at Capesthorne.

On 26 June 1838, Samuel married Mary Priscilla Needham of Lenton, Nottingham (who was the cousin of Samuel's sister-in-law, Mary Philips, wife of his eldest brother, Robert Hyde Greg). Samuel's wife, Mary, helped him in his work. They had 8 children; 6 daughters and 2 sons. Their eldest daughter, Amy Ellena, born 9 March 1840, later taught Martha Ann Wright at Lowerhouse Sunday School, (see the photograph of Amy and her elderly mother, Mary, using her ear trumpet). Three more daughters and one son were also born at Turner Heath.

During these early years Samuel took part in local affairs in Macclesfield. He was a Borough Magistrate and Vice-President and later President of the Useful Knowledge Society where he gave lectures.

Greg Family at The Mount

The Mount, Bollington
Built by Samuel Greg. His family moved here from Turner Heath in 1845

Miss Agnes Greg sitting outside The Mount.
Details of clothing and furniture are shown.
Ann Bennett was Lady's Maid to Miss Agnes

Miss Agnes and Miss Sally Greg, Samuel's older
sisters, outside The Mount showing grass in the
foreground. The front garden is reflected in the
window behind.

Samuel Greg (junior) 1804 – 1876

Mrs. Mary Greg (Samuel's widow) with ear trumpet and her eldest daughter, Miss Amy Greg.
They compiled "Layman's Legacy" in memory of Samuel Greg (junior) which was published in 1883.
Miss Amy's necklace would have cost about 2s-6d at the time
(Martha Ann Wright)

The growing family needed more space and Greg bought over 119 acres of land near Bollington Cross. In 1845 and 1846 Samuel studied farming operations on this land. On it he built a larger house on the hill and named it The Mount. Lowerhouse or Goldenthal (as he renamed it from a German fairy tale) lay in the valley below. (In 1851 census Lowerhouse is called Goldenthal). He took great care and interest in laying out the gardens around the house. Samuel donated land on which to build Bollington Cross School. which opened in 1845. The building was also used as a church. Their elder son, Samuel Herbert, was born 29 May 1846 at Turner Heath. In September 1846 the family moved into The Mount where two more daughters were born. Their younger son, Walter, was born 14 February 1851. On 5 April 1853 their second daughter, Hester, aged 11 years, died after a long illness. Mrs. Elizabeth Gaskell visited her friends, the Gregs at the Mount 1849 – 1850 and wrote some of her book "Mary Barton" here.

From the Bollington Map and Tithe Award 28 June 1848, Samuel Greg is listed as landowner of Lowerhouse - a total of over 13 acres, total tithes paid £15.16s.4d. Out of this total acreage, Greg was owner-occupier of two factory buildings and yard, pools, plantation, playground, school house and gardens; an area of over 4½ acres paying tithe of 6s.0d. Other tenants occupied the cottages and gardens, including Long Row, on 8½ acres of Greg's land, paying total tithes of £15.6s.4d. between them. Samuel Greg also owned and occupied 119 acres of untithed land around The Mount, owning another 10 acres of land occupied by tenants. Names from the Tithe Award and other sources have been added to the original Tithe Map 1849, which showed numbered plots only, to link it with the text.

 In 1846 Samuel introduced some new stretching machinery into the mill, which his workforce saw as a threat. Some of his workers came out on strike. Samuel was shattered by their attitude. He felt betrayed and feared that all the improvements made for workers in his model village community might be considered worthless by others. He suffered a nervous breakdown and abandoned the mill for good. For 30 years affairs were controlled by a mill manager and all business correspondence was sent to the mill. Samuel devoted his energies to the education of his family and to theological affairs, having always been a deeply religious man.

By 1847 Samuel had amassed business debts of around £32,000. His three brothers were eager to prevent him from being declared bankrupt and tried to pay his debts. Robert Hyde and John bought his estates shares to restore the mill to efficient profitability. William Rathbone Greg became manager at Lowerhouse until 1850, when his own mill at Bury deteriorated. He sold this and retired from business altogether. He then joined the Civil Service in London.

In 1850, John Greg of Caton, Lancaster, took over Lowerhouse Mill and continued to run it with his son, Francis, until John retired in 1864. Then Francis and his older brother, Albert, converted the mill into a private limited company. All the shareholders came from the family circles of Gregs, Rathbones and Melly families.

Samuel and Mary had to bring up their young family without a business income. To help the family, Samuel's older sister, Agnes Jane (5th child born 4 February 1797 died 1876, aged 79 years) came from Quarry Bank House, Styal, to live at The Mount in 1851. The house was divided into two, so that Miss Agnes then aged 54 years could have her own separate household. While living at Styal, Miss Agnes and Miss Sally Greg (Sarah, 6th child born 4 April 1798, died 17 January 1897, aged 99 years) worked with the poor girls in the Apprentice House. They taught needlework and domestic management and some girls went for short stays in Southport. Both sisters were thought to be pretentious. The 1861 census for Mount House Bench Lane, shows the Greg family and servants.

1861 Census Bollington

106 Mount House Bench Lane Bollington 2575/33 21

Greg Samuel Esq.	Head	m	56	Landed Proprietor	Ches. Wilmslow
Greg Mary	Wife	m	51		Notts. Lenton
Greg Bertha	Dau	unm	18		Ches. Bollington
Greg Alice	Dau	unm	16		Ches. Bollington
Greg Isobel	Dau	unm	11		Ches. Bollington
Greg Walter	Son	unm	10		Ches. Bollington
Lucas Frances	Servant	unm	21	Housemaid	Ches. Macclesfield
Thames Faith	Servant	unm	45	Cook	Notts. Tythby
*Greg Amy Ellena	Dau	unm	21	(not at home)	Ches. Bollington

Greg Agnes	Head	unm	64	Share Holder	Lancs Manchester
Ronalds -	Visitor	unm	24	Teacher	Middx. London
Greg John	Visitor	m.	59	County Magistrate Deputy Mayor of Lancaster Cotton Manufacturer	Ches. Wilmslow
Brogden Eliza	Servant	widow	58	Houseservant	Ireland
Bennett Ann	Servant	unm	23	Houseservant	Ches. Shrigley
Bennett Catherine	Servant	unm	28	Houseservant	Ches. Bollington

Burgess Joseph	Head	m	41	Coachman	Ches. Wilmslow
Burgess Mary	Wife	m	31		Ches. Macclesfield

164 Water Street

Warren Matthew	Head	mar	35	Grocer, Farmer 14 acres	Ches. Bollington
Warren Mary	Wife	mar	43	Grocer, Farmer's Wife	Ches. Rainow
Turner Thomas	Stepson		14	Joiner	Ches. Bollington
Turner Fredk.	Stepson		6	Scholar	Ches. Bollington
Warren Elizabeth	Daughter		5	Scholar	Ches. Bollington
Wright Alfred	Lodger	unm	17	Joiner	Ches. Rainow
Chislworth Rachel	Lodger	unm	19	Cotton Factory Worker	Ches. Bollington

Map of Bollington Cross and Lowerhouse

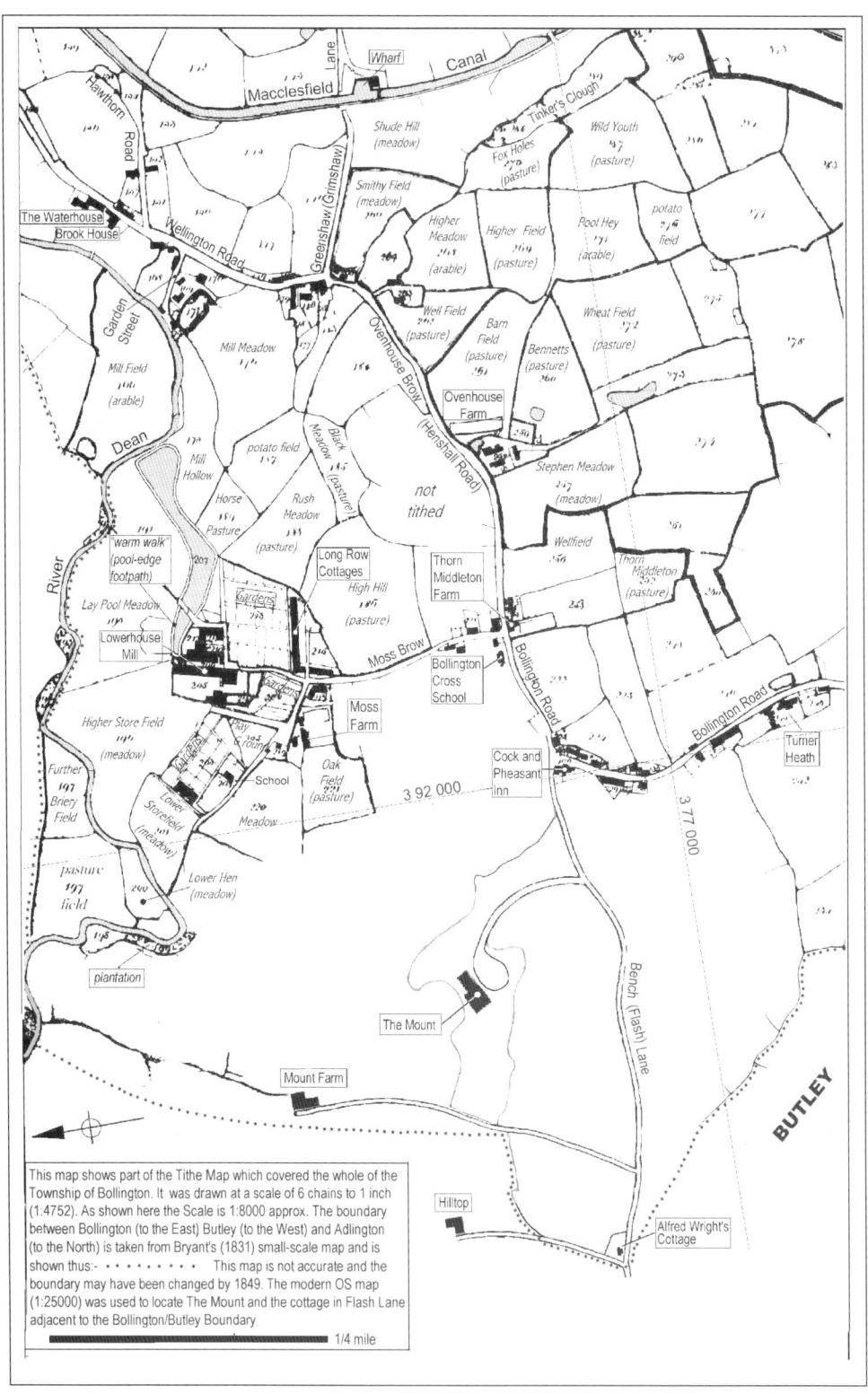

From Bollington Tithe Commutation Act Award: 28 June 1848

Owner	Occupier	Map No.	Land Use	Quantity			Tithe		
				A	R	P	£	s	d
Samuel Greg Esq (Lowerhouse)	Himself	199	Plantation	4	2	5	0	6	0
		204	School House & Gars						
		205	Play Ground						
		207	Pools						
		208	Factory & yard						
		209	Factory						
	James Ardern & others	202	Bank cottages	1	3	33	0	6	0
		203	Gardens						
	Martha Jones & others	206	Gardens	1	2	11	0	3	10
		210	Cott. Yards &						
		211	Gardens						
		212							
	James Dickenson & others	213	Gardens	4	2	27	0	15	0
		214	Long Row Cottages						
	Sam. Buckley & others	215	Gardens	0	1	25	0	1	6
	John Orme & others	216	Cottages						
	Roden Roach & others	217	Cottages	0	2	30			

List of lands merged or extinguished

Owner	Occupier	Quantity		
		Acres	Roods	Perches
Samuel Greg Esq. (Mount)	Himself	119	0	33
Samuel Greg Esq.	Rebecca Bancroft	0	0	33
	Thomas Welch	6	1	30
	James Hayes & others	0	0	29
	Samuel Linley	0	0	21
	Peter Pownall	3	2	17
	George Hill & others	0	1	28

Peace

By S. G. (Samuel Greg) written during the Crimea War

January 16th 1856   Camp before Sebastopol Crimea

Far over land and sea
From heaven's blue canopy
The moon looks down
O'er the dark and heaving main
O'er mountain rock and plain
And the walls of the ruined town.

She looks down from the sky
On the camp where thousands lie
In slumber deep
Each with his tent outspread
Each on a soldier's bed
Sleep a soldier's sleep.

And all is hushed and still
O'er mountain cave and hill
Through earth and sky
The pride and pomp of war
The banner trump and cry
In silence lie.

Hark this the still night air
Like the voice of a heartbreathed prayer
Wafted above
O'er the waves of the western sea
There comes a sweet voice to me
Like the voice of love.

Yes love! for it serves to say
As it dies on the air away
"Let there be peace"!
And a voice from the murmering waves
And a voice from the hollow caves
Replies, Peace! Peace! Peace!

The moon from her starry throne
Seems to say as she gazes down
Let war and carnage cease
And mountain shore and plain
Breathe back the word again
Peace! Peace! Peace!

The soldier lifts his head
He starts from lowly bed
To some strange sweet sound
He looks out upon the night
And he sees the calm pure light
Bathing the world around.

And a voice falls on his ear
Like some angel whispering near
Let there be peace
And mountain shore and plain
Echo the word again
Peace! Peace! Peace!

Now side by side they stand
Each sheathes his shining brand
The flag is furled
War, strife and carnage cease
And again the Star of Peace
Shines o'er the world.

A.E.S. November 18th 1860
Miss Ann Bennett
No 2, The Mount
Bollington.

Ann Bennett had become Lady's maid to Miss Agnes Greg by 4 February 1860 until 22 December 1864 when she married Alfred Wright at Prestbury Church. During her time as Lady's maid travelling with Miss Agnes, there are several references to Miss Sally Greg in the letters written from Mossley Hill, Liverpool, 4 July 1860, Escowbeck, Caton 13th August 1863. In her last letter of 31 October 1864 she tells her mother that Miss Sally, then aged 66 years, is frequently staying at The Mount and had been in bed with a bad cold, which Ann developed. Miss Sally was having the Barley Mow renovated. (It had been a public house and it was being made into a comfortable home for her. It was expected that she would bring William, her coachman, from Liverpool with her. Later the house was renamed Barley Grange.

Further information about Samuel Greg is available from "Laymans Legacy" - selections in prose and verse from the papers of Samuel Greg with a brief memoir compiled and edited by Samuel's widow, Mary P. Greg and daughter, Amy. (published 1883). Amy gave a copy to Martha Ann Wright, Ann Bennett's daughter. They describe Samuel Greg:

> *"as being small built, having a deep musically toned voice. He was a good speaker, popular, earnest, paying courtesy and respect to his audience. His noble thoughts inspired his hearers".*

Samuel was the centre and life of the community with a pleasant word for everyone. He taught a class in Sunday School. One of his Silver Cross girls said,

> *"He was a good man. There never was such a teacher of scripture".*
> *"A feature of the Greg family Sunday evening home life was that the whole household was assembled to hear Samuel's "reading". There were many regrets by old servants or the house when these readings came to an end".*

As Samuel recovered from his breakdown, he took up drawing and to write prose and poems. In 1852 the Sunday School Association published his "Stories from the Life of Jesus". He wrote the words of a hymn "Stay Master Stay upon this heavenly hill" (Hymns and Psalms No. 158) at The Mount on the hill overlooking Lowerhouse. Samuel was concerned about the Camp before Sebastopol and wrote his poem 'Peace' on 16 January 1856. His wife, Mary, wrote "Little Walter", a book of religious stories for young children, published in 1862.

Occasionally he joined his fellow magistrates on the Bench and he also wrote newspaper articles. He travelled to Italy with his wife and daughters in 1885. In the winter of 1867 he gave a course of scientific lectures to a class of boys at the Useful Knowledge Society. He later invited them to spend a summer evening at 'The Mount' and occasionally he invited members of his congregation to his home. They were very pleasant, cheerful evenings spent with his family in conversation varied with music, games or strolls in the grounds.

In June 1871 he had sudden heart trouble. He improved and was able to walk the local hills. By May 1875 he developed heart disease with breathing difficulties which lasted until his death on 14 May 1876. Widespread mutual respect was shown in flowers and letters of condolence.

> *"His funeral procession was met in Macclesfield by mill workers, civic dignitaries, members of the Useful Knowledge Society, clergymen and members of their congregations and friends. As the procession passed through town (Macclesfield) the flag on the old church (St. Michaels) was hoisted half mast. Men stood bareheaded on the pavement. The hearse entered the beautifully situated cemetery through double lines of sympathising faces. A service was held in the cemetery chapel at which Mr. Wright, an old friend, spoke. There was a peal of muffled bells from the old church."*

5

Samuel Wright

This chapter contains a selection of Samuel's handwritten poems from his book "Fallen Leaves" which is undated.

Old Nab

Old Nab, I now will sing thy praise,
For I have known thee all my days;
Thy noble and majestic form
Hath bravely weather'd ev'ry storm.

But when they've gather'd round thy head,
And devastation widely spread,
Conceal'd beneath the frozen snows,
Hast thou retired to have repose.

Through countless ages that are past,
Thou hast endured cold Winter's blast;
And keen has been the air, I trow,
As it has swept across thy brow.

But yet there have been brighter days,
When Spring, with its enliv'ning rays,
Has warm'd and, with refreshing showers,
Reviv'd again thy wasted powers.

With life and vigour thus inspired,
And in thy gayest robes attired,
How sweet it is at eventide
To sit upon thy flowery side.

To me thou art a pleasing sight;
In youth, I've viewed thee with delight
And now, in age, I will confess
I love to see thee none the less.

When far beyond the deep blue sea,
My thoughts have wander'd back to thee;
Have travers'd thy green pastures o'cr,
As I had done in days of yore.

With thy proud peak so grand and high,
Admired by each one passing by,
Surrounding hills will not compare;
Not even "Nancy", over there.

Poor "Billinge Head" and "Rainow Low"
But little claim to fame can show;
Though some may call them great and fine,
The palm, Old Nab, must still be thine.

Samuel Wright

Samuel, as a young father, describes their happy family life in his poem, here printed in a newspaper. Mary died suddenly on 10 September 1851, aged 34 years when their daughter Martha Ann was 10 and their son, Alfred, was 8 years old.

Samuel Wright, grocer and poet, photographed behind his shop, 8, Shrigley Road, Bollington (about 1860). Samuel was the elder, surviving twin, baptised 22 May 1814, died 5 February 1887. He married Mary Bradley on 23 January 1837.

OUR COTTAGE HOME.

The clouds now break, and heavy rains
Descend upon the window panes ;
The silv'ry moon withdraws her light,
And dark and cheerless is the night.
Whilst list'ning to the hollow sound
Of wintry winds that sport around,
How sad it is to think of those
Who know not where to find repose,
But homeless wand'ring all forlorn,
Wishing at night that it was morn,
Yet ere the morning's sun doth rise
They may in death have closed their eyes,
And thus their wretched lives they end
Uncared for and without a friend.
But we are safely sheltered here—
From outward storms we need not fear ;
In peace and quietness we share
Our Father's providential care,
And as our daily toil is o'er
We now will closely shut the door,
And take our well-appointed rest
Of all that we can do the best.
What social pleasures here we find !
What comfort and what peace of mind !
Shut in from ev'ry outward care,
A feast of happiness we share,
As snugly seated round the fire
We envy neither " lord nor squire,"
For, as our poets sometimes sing,
Riches but seldom bliss can bring.
Within this little homely cot
Contentment long has been our lot ;
Although our means may be but small,
Yet, thankful, we enjoy them all ;
Our Heavenly Father is so good
He gives us health and daily food,
And if He wealth to us denies
Whate'er is needful he supplies.
No more than this do we desire,
Save that He will our hearts inspire
To offer Him our humble praise,
And love and serve Him all our days.
We see our children round us play,
And pass their happy hours away ;
Whilst I my pipe sedately smoke
Their little heads I love to stroke :
Sitting in this old two-armed chair
I drive far from me ev'ry care,
And thus my weary limbs I rest
With joyous feelings in my breast.
And Mary with a smiling face
Beside the fire now takes her place ;
Her countenance benign and sweet
Makes all our comforts more complete,
For what is home, however fair,
Without a woman's tender care ?
Like a good angel she presides,
And ev'ry thought and action guides.
For happiness we need not roam,
Since we can have it here at home,
Aye, even in the humblest breast
She'll not disdain to be a guest.
Then come, thou sweet celestial maid,
And every bosom now pervade ;
O, come, that all may taste and see
How sweet it is to dwell with thee.

Shrigley-road, Bollington.   S. W.

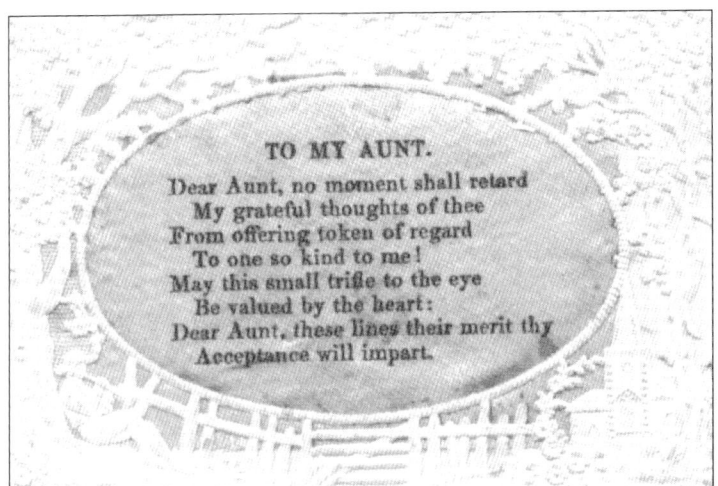

TO MY AUNT.

Dear Aunt, no moment shall retard
My grateful thoughts of thee
From offering token of regard
To one so kind to me!
May this small trifle to the eye
Be valued by the heart:
Dear Aunt, these lines their merit thy
Acceptance will impart.

Samuel wrote inside the card , "Presented to Pheby Ward by Martha Ann and Alfred Wright July 10th 1853".
It is likely that Aunt Pheby, Samuel's older sister, came to help him and the children until he married Ann Greenhalgh.

Memorial cards of Samuel Wright's family.

Samuel's wife, Mary (nee Bradley) died on 10 September 1851, at Dukinfield Hall, after a sudden illness. She was only 34 years old.

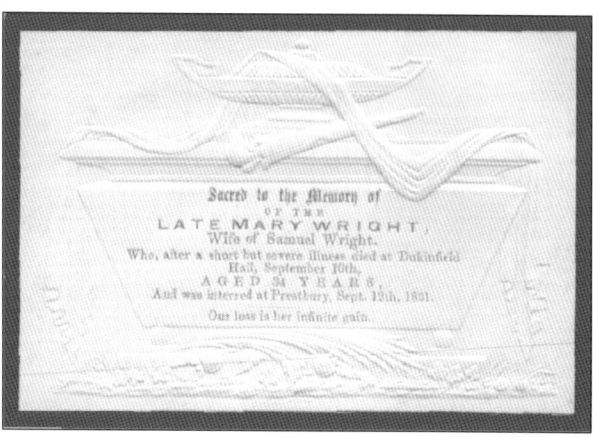

Samuel was devastated by the premature deaths of his wife and then his daughter in her 18th year, on 25 August 1858. Samuel wrote poems about these life-changing events.

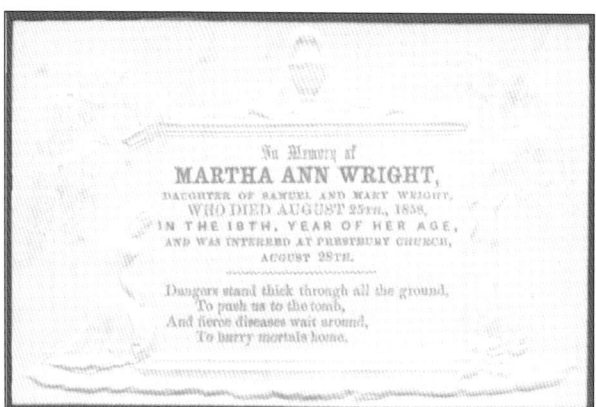

Samuel married Ann Greenhalgh on 30 July 1853 and lived until his 73rd year. Samuel's memorial card, 5 February 1887.

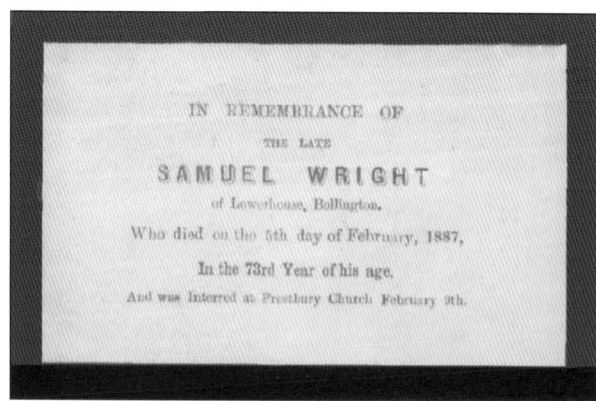

All are buried in Prestbury Churchyard. In the 1850s, memorial cards were embossed. The width of the black borders indicated the importance of the person. By the 1870s, memorial cards were folded with details given inside.

White Nancy (extracts)

We see White Nancy all alone,
Though she by all is so well-known;
Her old white dress, which she has worn
For ages, makes her look forlorn.
Dame Fashion, with her freaks so strange,
On this old lady makes no change;
For she, as people mostly know,
Is what she was long years ago…………..

But as to what may be her age,
Does not appear on history's page;………
And Nancy's age we cannot find.
All that we learn when we enquire,
Is that a certain country squire
Posess'd of wealth and mod'rate skill
And dwelt, 'tis said, at Tower Hill,
Conceived the thought, till then unknown,
Of placing Nancy on a throne………….
But Northern Nancy still remains,
And all her stateliness retains;
Her plain but ancient looking form
Still braves the fury of the storm………….

But see this old and batter'd door,
How it is cut and chequer'd o'er;
What proud initials, and what names
Of people whose ambitious aims
Have brought them here that they might scan
The beauties of old Northern Nan.
From close beside her whitewash'd walls,
Far off are seen the stately halls………….

But O how glorious is the scene;
All nature is arrayed in the green;
For miles and miles the country round
Is everywhere with beauty crown'd.
The rising hills on every hand,
That such extensive views command,
The meadows lying down below,
And all the little streams that flow,
The verdant trees, the varied flowers,
Refresh'd by gently falling showers,
To Thee, great Lord of all, they raise
Their silent ceaseless hymn of praise.

White Nancy, showing the door and window.

On passing Shrigley Church

As now I pass the village church,
I gaze upon its form;
And think how long it must have stood
The fury of the storm.

The many dangers it has pass'd,
When dark has been the day;
And yet through all hath been preserv'd
From sinking to decay.

And as in ages now gone by,
May this old fabric stand;
The joy of every British heart,
The glory of our land.

I love to see its ancient tower,
Its bells, how sweet they sound;
Each Sabbath day the villagers
Assembled here are found.

And here beneath the hallow'd sod,
How many sleeping lie,
Who worshipp'd in this grey old pile,
The God of earth and sky?

And shall not we with reverent awe,
The same old path pursue;
Leave all the cares of this vain world,
We now are passing through?

For we, like them, shall pass away.
Shall die and be forgot;
These bells may ring as sweetly then,
But we shall hear them not.

May all who meet within these walls
To pay their vows to Thee,
Receive thy blessing and, O Lord,
For good remember me.

Dear Brother

My friends and neighbours all agree
In what they think concerning me
And tell me with a serious air
That I am getting worse for wear

They say it gives them quite enough
To see me breathe, and hear me cough
And, so advise me to beware
For I am getting worse for wear.

And I myself am much inclined
To be of their sagacious mind
Because my feelings witness bear
That I am much the worse for wear.

I have a rattling at my breast
Which often robs me of my rest
And of a cure I do despair
Because I'm so much worse for wear.

I'm also very much oppress'd
With indigestion at my chest
Which greatly doth my health impair
And make me feel the worse for wear.

And when I eat my daily food
The mastication is not good
For want of teeth to grind and tear
Another proof I'm worse for wear.

And if I reach that heavenly shore
I then will view my journey o'er
And praise My God for being there
And having done with worse for wear.

Samuel Wright

Dear Brother,

Today I feel considerably better. I breathe better in consequence of the air being so much clearer; I would like to continue so for believe me, I am getting rather tired of an idle life, to say nothing of what I am losing in a pecuniary point of view, hoping that you are all enjoying health at Bollington – And that Mrs Sharpley is got perfectly restored.

I remain Dear Brother
Your affectionate Brother

Sam.L Wright

I should like to know why Alfred does not write to me a little oftener.

S.W.

Written by Samuel to his youngest brother, Isaac Wright, then grocer at 8 Shrigley Road and living at Pear Tree Cottage. Samuel's 15 year old son Alfred was an apprentice joiner. Samuel was recovering from a chest infection 3 months after his 17 year old daughter's premature death. Mrs. Sharpley was their sister Esther, who came to help Isaac when his first wife died following the birth of their second daughter in 1851.

To Mrs A.W.*

The tidings I am glad to hear
That you are now restor'd to health;
And that another little dear
Has just been added to your wealth.

May heaven preserve the darling child,
Fond object of its mother's love,
As lovely and as undefiled
As angels are who live above.

And may its tender life be spared,
And, day by day, may grace be given,
That he may be by it prepared
To live on earth the life of heaven.

But if, perchance, through Adam's fall,
He should partake of toil and care,
May God, who is so good to all,
Keep him from ev'ry evil snare.

Walking in wisdom's pleasant ways,
Upright and truthful and sincere;
May he be lov'd through all his days,
By all who know him far and near.

In all the slipp'ry paths of youth,
And up to manhood's full estate,
O may he ever keep the truth,
And strive to be both wise and great.

But this, perhaps, I may not see,
Since I am daily growing old;
For when your child a man shall be,
My fourscore years will all be told.

But it shall be my constant prayer
That God will all your children save;
And watch o'er them with tender care,
When I am mould'ring in my grave.

*Mrs AW is the wife of Alfred Wright, Ann (née Bennett) Samuel's daughter in law.
(Lady's Maid 1860-64 to Miss Agnes Greg at The Mount, Bollington)

My dear Niece[1],

I am taking it upon me to send you a few lines in writing and in doing so I can assure you that I am activated by no other motive than that of love and a desire to fulfil a duty imposed upon me by your father[2] a short time before he died. At present I know you are busily engaged in getting ready to go into your new house[3], and, cannot but congratulate you on having such a house to go to for I am sure you will agree with me when I say that is in every respect an ornament to the village and I sincerely hope that when you have removed to it you will feel comfortable and at home.

But whilst I have been thinking over these things a little incident has occurred to my mind which took place about a hundred years ago. It relates to your good old grandmother[4] who used to live at Pott Shrigley[5]. Some thirty or forty years since I was told by one of the oldest persons in Adlington that when your grandmother was a young women - she had not the equal for beauty in all that township, and what was infinitely better in early life she gave her heart to God and became a member of the Methodist Society. On receiving her first "ticket" that great and good man Dr Townley solemnly addressed her in these works, "Mary, take care that no one takes they crown". This she remembered as long as she lived and was wise enough to act upon the advise given. She took care and I have no doubt but that she is now wearing her crown in heaven. Well I thought what a pity it will be if this fine house with all its beautiful surroundings and the company with which you will perhaps have to associate should take your crown. I do not say that it will be so, I hope it will not but I do say that there will be great danger and therefore I earnestly entreat you to take care, whatever you do take care.

I am your Affectionate Uncle

Samuel Wright

PS This communication is unknown to any one but you and myself, let it remain so but be sure you think seriously on what I have said. S.W.

---

[1] *Mary Wright b 18 Sept 1854 m Tom Jackson*

[2] *Isaac Wright 1818 - 22 Sept 1875*

[3] *Brook Bank", Wellington Road – sold 1933 for BUDC Council Offices and renamed Town Hall in 1980. "Brook Bank" was built for Tom Jackson and Mary (nee Wright) by Tom's father as a wedding present. Tom and his father were bankers in Manchester, who travelled there daily by steam train from Bollington Station. From the ledgers of Arighi Bianchi Macclesfield, there are records of Tom and Mary buying furniture for their new home.*

[4] *Mary Lane, Richard Wright's wife b. 1776, d. 1852*

[5] *Woodbine Cottage*

6

Martha Ann Wright's Personal Recollections.

I tape recorded Grandma Wright's vivid recollections of her early life in 1963 for the first Bollington Festival in l964. Later, in 1991, I put them and other family history stories into book form for my grandsons and the Macclesfield Silk Heritage Education Section.

Martha Ann spoke of Samuel Greg and his family, The Mount and Lowerhouse with great respect and affection. She heard her parents speak of them and knew them personally as she had lived at Lowerhouse in the 1880s. Her mother, Ann Bennett, had been Lady's maid to Miss Agnes Greg (Samuel's sister) at The Mount from 1860 until 1864 when she married Alfred Wright, joiner at Lowerhouse Mill and The Mount, on 22 December 1864 at Prestbury Church.

Martha Ann was their second child and only daughter, among six brothers, born 1 September 1868, died 3. May 1969.   The Wright family first lived in a cottage at the bottom of Flash Lane in the corner of Samuel Greg's land. Sweet briar and honeysuckle grew round the casement window. In the garden was a spring with a stone sink below, from which they obtained fresh water. Alfred made the children a wooden horse called 'Black Bess' which they pulled up and down the garden. He hung a swing from the russet apple tree. They kept a cow called 'Blossom' which gave them milk. For a time they kept a few hens and a pig. Their large firegrate with a side oven was cleaned with black lead. Ann was a good mother and excellent needlewoman, who made all the children's clothing, coats and hats, besides looking after her family and home. Alfred, her father, was a good joiner who would only use wood with a good grain and his name was stamped on all his tools. He was asked to make furniture for the Greg home at The Mount.   He made a similar dresser to one made for the Gregs to keep the children's clothing and household linen in for their own cottage. He earned a wage of 29s. 6d. a week.

As Greg employees, Ann and Alfred visited The Mount, sometimes with their children. Martha Ann remembers being invited to The Mount for the Greg's Christmas distribution, to see their decorated Christmas tree, a holly bush from the garden. They were given small presents from it. Martha Ann was given a small bellows made of black and white check silk. It had pins round it and a long pin for the spout. She kept it carefully for years, but her older brother, Charles, soon broke his present!

Charles, their eldest son born in 1865, seems to have been hyperactive. The Family Bible records that "Charles Wright from Christmas 1869 to May 1870 was afflicted with the Lumbar Abscess so severely that his life was despaired of at the age of $4^{1}/_{2}$ years". Aged 9 years, Charles was a pupil at a school in Lostock Terrace, Poynton, living nearby with his elderly grandparents, Charles and Jane Bennett (teacher) at Hope Green where Aunt Mary Bennett cared for them.

Alfred and Ann Wright's Family Bible

This large, leather-bound, gold-tooled, illustrated book was a wedding present from Ann's sister, Mary Bennett, dated 22 December 1864. This page records their dates of birth, marriage and death. The surrounding border shows pictures of the stages of life.

Alfred and Ann lived in half of this cottage in Flash Lane Bollington. Built on the corner of Samuel Greg's land at the Mount, the public footpath (and drive to Hilltop) runs past the gable-end.

Charles, Martha Ann, Philip, Hedley and John were all born here, 1865 – 1874. Samuel was born in 1877 in Water Street, Bollington and George at Lowerhouse in 1881.

1871 Census Bollington

Flash Lane

Wright Alfred	Head	mar	27	Joiner, Carpenter	Cheshire Rainow
Wright Ann	Wife	mar	33	Cheshire Shrigley	
Wright Martha Ann	Daughter		2	Cheshire Bollington	
Wright Philip	Son		2 months	Cheshire Bollington	
Bennett Mary	Sister in Law	unm	36	Lately Servant	Cheshire Macclesfield

Charles Wright, their eldest child, born 19 November 1865, aged 5½ , is not at home on the night of the census 3 April 1871. Neither are his grandparents at Hope Green, Adlington. One wonders whether they had taken Charles away on holiday, as they are not in the whole area of Macclesfield and district. Charles had almost lost his life from the lumbar abscess at 4½, from Dec 1869 to May 1870.

Mary Bennett, Ann's elder sister, was helping Ann after Philip's birth.

Bollington Methodist Church attended by the Wright family.

Bollington Cross and Greg Fountain

The Greg Fountain was opened in 1904 in memory of the Greg family

The fountain seat was well used on warm days, by local men who met there for a chat.

Bollington Cross Church of England School (pre 1908).

Built on land donated by Samuel Greg, the school opened in 1845. The building with a porch, bell tower and ecclesiastical windows was also used as a church for 63 years until St Oswald's Church was opened in 1908. The school was extended in this year.

The Greg family drove out in a horse and carriage called a Phaeton. Burgess was the coachman. He also filled the coal buckets for the fires and other jobs to help the other servants. In the early 1870's, Martha Ann remembered seeing ladies from The Mount wearing 'hunting pink', as they rode horses across Mount Farm fields behind their cottage.

Most people from Bollington area were buried at Prestbury and funerals passed their cottage. It was a 'great event' for the children and they ran to the garden gate to watch the procession of mourners pass by. Men wore tall silk hats with black silk bands and ribbon tails which hung down to the shoulders. The hearse and carriages were drawn by horses.

Martha Ann attended Bollington Cross Day School where her infant teacher was Miss Hough. As their growing family outgrew the cottage in Flash Lane, they first moved into a shop in Water Street on the opposite corner of John Street and Wesleyan Methodist Sunday and Day School. Samuel was born here on 21 May 1877. The older children and Martha Ann attended the Wesleyan Sunday School in Water Street during this time. They are recorded in the attendance register 1876-8 and on Martha Ann's Sunday School Prize label 12th. March 1880.

Alfred built the house, shop and workshop in 1880 in Moss Brow, Lowerhouse, where George was born on 10th July 1881. Martha Ann was almost 13 years old and had left Day School. As the only girl in the family Martha Ann helped her mother in the house and shop.

Lowerhouse shop opened one Friday evening in 1881. Martha Ann's grandfather was Samuel Wright, grocer and poet. He made up $1/2$ ounces of tobacco ready for sale. The first customer was Patsy Murphy. Martha Ann ran in to serve him a $1/2$ oz tobacco. Alfred grumbled at her saying that customers didn't want to be served by a child! She was about 13 years old.

Her mother, Ann Bennett, made four dozen lbs. of flour daily into bread and plain cakes. People from the mill came to buy a plain cake spread with butter and 2 oz cheese between, for their lunch. Martha Ann made teacakes on Thursdays and Fridays and sold them. That was her money. Betsy Wood made humbugs at home by pinching them into 3 cornered shapes with her fingers. They were called Wilmslow humbugs. She lived at the cottage at the end of Farm Lane. (Moss Lane).

Baby George died aged 20 months on 17 March 1883. Ann made a black mourning dress for Martha Ann ($14^1/_2$ years) to wear at the funeral. It affected Alfred deeply to make a small coffin for his son. For besides being a joiner, Alfred made coffins and had some ready for use in his workshop. Martha Ann helped to line coffins with white satin.

When Samuel Greg retired from the mill, Mr. Francis of Turner Heath, Bollington Cross, Mr. Albert from Caton near Lancaster and Mr. Hugh (Mr. Albert's son) came to learn the business. They had lunch with Martha Ann's family three mornings a week.

There was an "Annual Dinnering" for the work people to which the Gregs came. Whittaker's shop (Mrs. Emily A Gardiner, nee Whittaker) provided the food. Wright's shop and off-licence provided beer and drink. Greg's speech told work people how trade was at the mill. There was a soup kitchen for the work people when times were bad in the Cotton Famine

Lowerhouse was a model village, like Styal. George Mayers garden behind the playground was beautiful. People walked down to see it on Sunday evenings. There was a school, library and Mill manager's house. Martha Ann remembers seeing books with 'Goldenthal Library' stamped inside them. The library was well used and every quarter it had an auction sale of magazines and graphics like Titbits, etc. Pictures of Cherry Ripe and Bubbles were given with magazines at Christmas as a special offer.

Infant George Wright's death

Infant George Wright's Memorial card, 17 March 1883.

Ann Wright (nee Bennett). Aged 45 years.
Wearing her black mourning dress after
George's death.

Martha Ann Wright. Aged 14½ years.
Wearing the black dress made for the funeral
of her baby brother George

Both dresses were made by Ann, and 5 months after the funeral are worn with white collars for the photographs. Alfred, Ann and Martha Ann had one week's holiday in Blackpool, in August 1883, just before Alfred with his two elder sons, Charles and Philip, sailed to New Zealand.

Both photographs were taken by E. Brook, photographer in Blackpool.

Lowerhouse (Goldenthal), Bollington

Moss Brow with house, shop and joinery work shop built by Alfred Wright in 1880

Moss Farm (in background), Whittaker's Cottage and Shop (on right) and Playground with swings in front.

Whittaker's Cottage (on left) with Shop attached. In the middle background is the Day and Sunday School on Moss Lane. The swings in the playground are on the right

Martha Ann attended Lowerhouse Sunday School where Miss Amy Greg taught her. The children sat round tables, six a side, writing with pen and ink. Her copybook contains the hymn or poem copied weekly which was learnt for the following week. During their holidays, Miss Amy's nieces (Dowsons from Gee Cross) visited Lowerhouse School. They wore blue llama frocks with white diaper pinafores over them. Martha Ann's younger brothers attended Lowerhouse Day School. Miss Cross and Miss Ellis were the teachers.

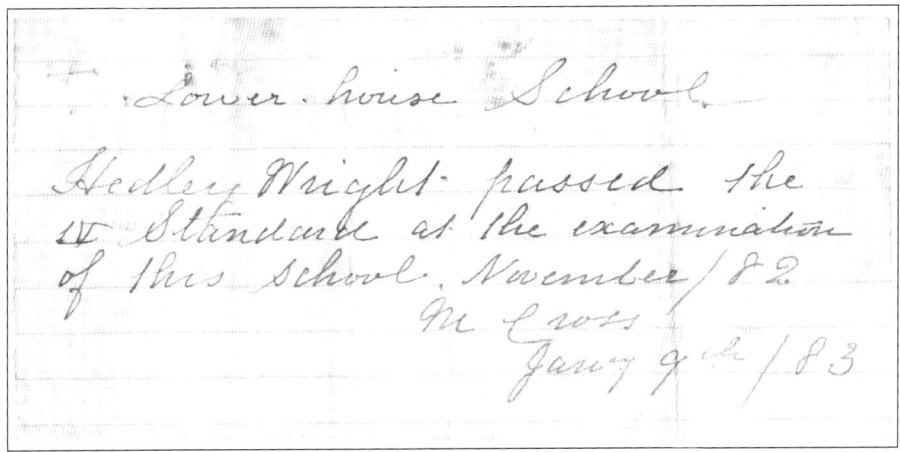

Lowerhouse School Certificate. Hedley was 10 years old.

Drinking water was drawn from two wells, one at the end of Farm Lane where you went up five steps to the well. The one at the other end of the lane was at ground level. Lowerhouse mill pond had warm water in it and was called the "warm walk", later called the "rope walk", where ropes were dried. The pond had gold and red fish together with lots of tadpoles and frogs in it. Yellow and white water lilies grew on it. There was a hot water tank at the mill which people could use for washday. Martha Ann had two large buckets which had previously contained lard from the shop. She had an iron yoke to carry the buckets - one each side. She climbed a ladder to reach water out of the tank. Sometimes a man worker might help her lift the heavy buckets down the ladder and onto the yoke. Lowerhouse and Moss Brow roads were swept every Saturday morning by labourers from Lowerhouse Mill.

The District Nurse was Mrs. Hannah Warburton. She looked after the sick and called the Doctor. She earned 5/- a week. Every cottage paid 3d. a week to the doctor so no bills were sent.

The playground had two sets of swings - four in all. There was a wooden donkey to ride on or jump over. The roundabout had chains on it and you held on and swung round it. On Good Fridays and in Wakes week, children from Macclesfield walked to Bollington to play on the playground as a special treat. The playground was locked up each Saturday evening in readiness for Sunday. Every Bollington Wakes Monday the organ grinder came to Lowerhouse. Sometimes he brought a monkey. Young people paid him and danced sets in the opening. They gave him more money to keep on playing for their dancing.

"O Shepherd rest; nor further go—
Thy tempest hath begun."
"I cannot stay, I must away
To find my wand'ring one!"

A thorn-wreath bound the gentle brow
That beamed with pity sweet;
And marks of wounds were on his hands,
And scars were on his feet.
Again I said "O Shepherd, rest;
Thine tempest hath begun!"
He murmured, "Nay, I must away
To find my wandring one!"

"I saw Thy flock at peace within
Thine own well-guarded fold;
O Shepherd pause: for wild the gale
That rages o'er the world!"
No; one has wandered far away,
And soon may be undone;
I cannot stay, I must away
To find my wandering one!"

Page from Martha Ann Wright's copybook.
Written at Lowerhouse Sunday School in the 1880s

Some of Samuel Greg's friends emigrated to New Zealand and wrote of better opportunities there. These glowing reports influenced Alfred Wright, after his infant son Geaorge's death in March 1883. The cotton trade fluctuated at Lowerhouse Mill and workers were laid off. This in turn affected Alfred's work as a joiner. Current local newspapers advertised emigration with cheap fares for key workers like joiners needed in New Zealand.

During the summer of 1883 Alfred and Ann decided that Alfred aged 40, would take 18 year old Charles and Philip aged 12 years by sailing ship from London to New Zealand. If successful the rest of the family could follow later. Before leaving at the end of August 1833 Alfred, Ann and Martha Ann shared a week's holiday together in Blackpool, where their photographs were taken to mark this "rite of passage". Their sons' photographs were taken locally. (Details of their adventures follow in the chapters on emigration). Life was tough in New Zealand and Alfred and Philip returned home by steamship "Ruapehu" which arrived in London on 4th January 1885. Charles remained in Auckland where he married and had one son.

At home Ann became ill and her sister Mary Bennett came to help care for her. Ann died of cancer on 18 April 1886. She was buried in Poynton Churchyard with the rest of her Bennett family. Miss Amy Greg wrote an empathic letter of condolence to Martha Ann and sent her a white satin ribbon bookmark for an Easter greeting, and other short notes in the 1890s. Alfred's elderly father Samuel Wright and stepmother Ann (nee Greenhalgh) died within 3 weeks of each other in January and February 1887. On 4th May 1887, Alfred married neighbour Martha Gardiner of Moss Farm, at Prestbury Church. Martha Ann said "we got on remarkably well stepmother and I". Before Martha Ann's letter 2 March 1889, Alfred and "some of her brothers had gone abroad". Samuel followed later. They sailed by steamship to Canada.

Martha Ann and Richard Wright, grocer and corn merchant of 13 – 15 Shrigley Road married at Bollington Wesleyan Methodist Church on 18 October 1893. They had delayed their summer wedding hoping that Alfred would return home to give his daughter away. To Martha Ann's disappointment none of her close family were present at their wedding (and are not on the group photograph). Her stepmother's brother John Gardiner of Mount Farm Bollington gave her away and his young son Ellis was page boy. Martha Ann wore a rose coloured silk poplin dress (donated to Macclesfield Silk Museum collection). The bridesmaids were Richard's sisters Edith and Martha. They wore dresses made of a new course material called hopsack in grey check, trimmed with dark purple velvet.

Richard and Martha Ann and bridesmaids drove from Church to Lowerhouse in Challinor's horse drawn cabs. On the way home they were "roped" by workmen, who were given money to allow them to pass. Albert Road (constructed 1868) was hung with garlands by neighbours. Alfred's joinery workshop adjoining the house had been cleared, scrubbed and the walls papered. Carpets were laid on the floor and curtains hung at the windows. In the evening guests sang two popular songs of the day "Two little girls in blue" and "Tarara-Boom-de-aye".

Richard Wright and Martha Ann lived in the house next to the grocery and corn merchant shop 13/15 Shrigley Road with his elderly mother Ellen (nee Whipp). Richard's father, Isaac Wright had built the row of cottages 13 – 19 in the 1870s. He transferred his grocery business there from the shop at the bottom of the hill 8 Shrigley Road which his brother Samuel took over. Richard's unmarried sisters and younger brother, Isaac Thomas Wright lived at 17 and 19 Shrigley Road.

Alfred and Ann Wright's sons; brothers to Martha Ann

Charles Wright c. 1874, scholar at
Lostock Hall School, Poynton. b. 19
November 1865

Philip Wright as a young man b. 8
February 1871.

Hedley Wright as a teenager, with
Rover. b. 8 October 1872

John and Samuel Wright in 1887. b. 3
December 1874 & 21 May 1877

Also, George, b. 10 July 1881, died in infancy on 17 March 1883 at home,
Moss Brow, Lowerhouse, Bollington

Memorial Card
Ann Wright (nee Bennett) – former Lady's Maid.

Inside the card is a verse and
details of Ann's death.

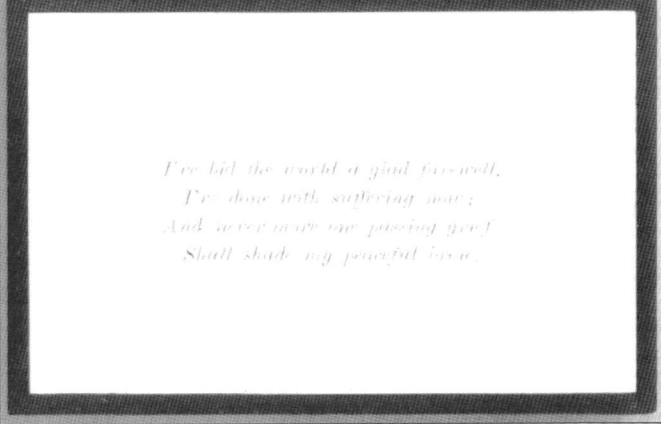

In Loving Memory of

ANN,

The beloved wife of Alfred Wright, of Lower Houses,
Bollington,

Who Died April 18th, 1886, Aged 48 Years.

And was Interred at Pexton Church, April 22nd.

Amy Greg's letter of condolence – 21 April 1886

Nottingham
Wedy.
April 21st
1886

My dear Martha,

I have only heard today that your poor Mother is at last released from her pain. I am sure the first great feeling with you all will be also one of relief, & thankfulness, to think that she is no longer suffering. for the first time for all these long sad months! but is free from the body, & able we hope. to rejoice & to rest. Then will come the wondering what sort of world she is in — what she

her closed eyes can see, & her ears hear, that ours cannot see & hear. And soon will come over you all the sad realization of the fact that you are motherless, in this world. that she is gone! May it help to draw you all nearer, dear Martha, to the Heavenly Father, who knows what a Mother's love is — & who knows what you will all miss in losing it.

You have had a very trying time of nursing — you, & your father especially, & your Aunt. I hope none of you have suffered seriously in health from it? & that you will be able to get rested, when this week is over. You will

Written to Martha Ann Wright on the death of her mother,
Ann, their former lady's maid – April 1886.

have, I hope, some happy, comfortable years to look back upon, before your mother was ill. & you will have learnt from her how to make your father & the rest comfortable at home, in the future. You have an important work depending on you, have you not — & I hope the boys will all know how to prize you & take care of you, in return for all you do for them! You will all be anxious to do & be what your mother would have wished — May God help you, & be with you, & be your Comforter, dear Martha — The

thoughts & services of Easter, if you are able to join in any of them, may be some solace to you — Please remember me very kindly to your father. I do not know when the funeral is to be — but I wished to write to you at once, as I do not go home till Saturday.

Believe me yours
very truly Amy Greg.

Amy had lost her father, Samuel Greg, ten years earlier and was
Martha Ann's teacher at Lowerhouse Sunday School.

Nottingham
Wed.
April 21st 1886

My Dear Martha,

      I have only heard today that your poor Mother is at last released from her pain. I am sure the first great feeling with you all will be also one of relief and thankfulness to think that she is no longer suffering for the first time for all these long sad months but is free from the body, and able we hope to rejoice and to rest. Then will come the wondering what sort of world she is in – what her closed eyes can see and her ears hear, that ours cannot see and hear. And soon will come over you all the sad realization of the fact that you are motherless, in this world that she is gone! May it help to draw you all nearer, dear Martha, to the Heavenly Father, who knows what a Mother's love is and who knows what you will all miss in losing it.

      You have had a very trying time of nursing – you and your father especially, and your Aunt. I hope none of you have suffered seriously in health from it? And that you will be able to get rested, when this week is over. You have, I hope, some happy comfortable years to look back upon, before your Mother was ill and you will have learnt from her how to make your father and the rest comfortable at home, in the future. You have an important work depending on you, have you not and I hope the boys will know how to prize you and take care of you, in return for all you do for them You will all be anxious to do and be what your Mother would have wished. May God help you and be with you, and be your Comforter, dear Martha. The thoughts and services of Easter, if you are able to join in any of them, may be some solace to you. Please remember me very kindly to your father. I do not know when the funeral is to be – but I wished to write to you at once, as I do not go home till Saturday.

Believe me yours,
Very truly,

Amy Greg

Easter and Christmas Greetings from Amy Greg to Martha Ann Wright

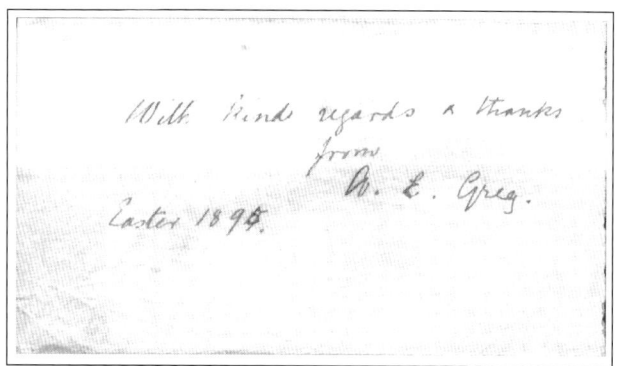

Easter bookmark in white satin with greetings.
Easter 1895

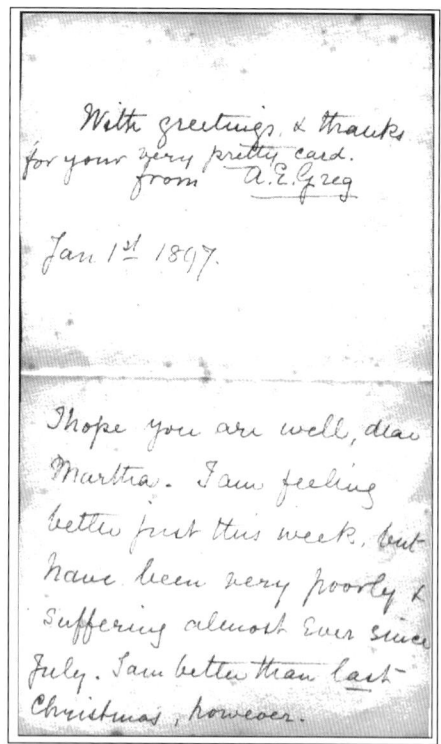

New Year greetings note
1st January 1897

Amy Greg and Martha Ann continued to keep in touch. These notes were treasured carefully by Martha Ann, Amy's former pupil at Lowerhouse Sunday School. In October 1893 she married Richard Wright, grocer and corn merchant of 13/15, Shrigley Road, Bollington.

Martha Wright (nee Gardiner) 1845 - 1910

Martha Gardiner was Alfred Wright's second wife, married 4 May 1887.

Martha was the second daughter of Charles and Jane Gardiner (nee Ainsworth) who farmed at Moss Farm, Lowerhouse. There were also three sons.

Mary the eldest daughter, married Henry Whittaker and kept the other grocers shop at Lowerhouse near the playground.

Their daughters were lifelong friends of Martha Ann Wright.

Martha Ann Wright's belated letter to Mr. & Mrs. Brooks, dated March 2 1889. In it she tells them of her mother's and grandparents' deaths and that her father and brothers had gone to Canada

Wedding of Richard Wright and Martha Ann Wright
18 October 1893

These photographs were taken outside the house and shop, Moss Brow, Lowerhouse. The reception was held in the joiners workshop (off right of photo). Richard's family only are shown as Martha Ann's father and brothers were in Canada and New Zealand and her mother had died.

All ten of the late Isaac Wright's children were present at the wedding, the small attendants were Jessie and Nellie daughters of John and Elizabeth Wright:- *(the numbers in brackets denote order of birth)*

Back row: - John(5), Martha(4), John Gardiner (gave the bride away)
2nd row: - Jane Ellen(6), Isaac Thomas(10), Mary Bennett, Mary(3), Elizabeth(2)
Sitting: - Esther Ann(1), Edith(9), Bertha(8), Martha Ann, Richard(7), Ellen (Isaac's 2nd wife), Martha (Martha Ann's stepmother)

A more informal picture (without hats). Ringed are the ten Wrights, together with Ellen (Richard's mother) and Martha Ann.

Wright Homes

9 – 15 Shrigley Road Bollington. Houses and shop built by Isaac Wright (grocer) for his growing family. Richard and Martha Ann Wright and their children continued as grocers and corn merchants.

Clifford, Leslie and Mary were born here.

Front parlour of No. 13 (photo by Isaac Thomas Wright who superimposed himself)

Woodbine Cottage, Pott Shrigley – home of John and Elizabeth Wright and their children, Jessie, Frederick and Nellie.

Richard transferred the growing corn business to the mill in Watson's Yard off High Street, Bollington and later to Prestbury Corn Mill behind St Peter's Church. Generations of the Wright family from Richard Wright (1776 – 1863) are listed in the Bollington Wesleyan Methodist church seat rent books 1837 – 1940. These date from the opening of the second chapel which had box pews and the present third chapel which was dedicated in 1886. The first chapel opened in 1808 on land given by Peter Lomas. Isaac Wright was appointed class leader in 1866. The family continued as class leaders, trustees and lifelong members.

Richard died in February 1926 and was buried in Pott Shrigley Churchyard. Martha Ann and Mary ran the grocer's shop, where Martha Ann opened a haberdashery section. Their sons Clifford and Leslie took over Prestbury Corn Mill, renamed Exors. of R Wright. The mill accidentally burnt down in March 1940 and had to be rebuilt. After Leslie's death in August 1940, Clifford ran the business alone. He sold the corn business and mill to Hamlyn's in November 1946.

Martha Ann Wright aged 90 years visited her brothers and their families in Canada in June 1958, and was accompanied by her daughter Mary and husband Albert Weate. After retiring from the business, these three continued to live together first in Macclesfield and then in a new bungalow in Tytherington.

Martha Ann celebrated her 100th birthday there on 1st September 1968. There was a family celebration dinner and much local interest for Martha Ann was a much loved, well known and respected lady. The Over Alderley Band cam to play her favourite hymns in their garden. Martha Ann had raised money for Church funds all her life and was an active member at Bollington and in the Macclesfield Methodist Circuit.

She had kept all her faculties and played the piano to the end. Her doctor said *'she was a very fortunate lady without a disease in her body'*. She died within a fortnight on 3 May 1969 from a cold which turned to pneumonia. She was buried in her husband Richard's and son Leslie's grave at Pott Shrigley Church after a Thanksgiving Service in Bollington Methodist Church.

Richard's brothers, sisters and cousins in England visited each other regularly all their lives. Edith and Simeon Robinson and their sons lived in Church Lawford, Rugby, Isaac Thomas, Sarah and family in Birkenhead and Heswall. Martha Ann's brother Philip and Edith and son Norman lived in Stockport. Her brothers who emigrated to New Zealand and Canada exchanged letters and there were rare visits. Their descendants are indicated with a 'v' on the family tree extract.

Martha Ann Wright 1 September 1868 – 3 May 1969

Martha Ann, aged 6 years,
wearing a yellow frock trimmed with blue
made by her mother.

Martha Ann, aged c.21 years,
wearing a brown velvet blouse.

Richard and Martha Ann Wright,
early1900s.

Martha Ann, 100 years old.

7

Emigration to New Zealand in the 1880s

Martha Ann Wright's chest of family papers contained original letters from her father, Alfred Wright and her brothers Charles and Philip who emigrated to New Zealand in 1883.

Alfred Wright, 1843-1898, was the only son of Samuel Wright and Mary, nee Bradley, who died when Alfred was 8 years old. He was a joiner and cabinet maker working at Lowerhouse Mill and Samuel Greg's home 'The Mount', Bollington

Alfred had heard glowing reports of life in New Zealand from the Gregs, who had friends who had emigrated, and they said how badly joiners were needed. No doubt Alfred read the notices on the front of the local weekly newspaper 'Macclesfield Courier' where there were many 'adverts' for emigration, shown overleaf.

Sail was the cheapest means of transport but it could take 9 months to a year to complete the round trip from Britain to Australia and New Zealand and back, circumnavigating the world using the prevailing winds. Clippers like the 'Cutty Sark' were specially designed for speed and took 60-70 days each way. It is remarkable that so many ships reached their destination safely for they were often in greatest danger when near land. It was difficult in stormy weather to keep the sailing ship away from the rocks and from being blown against the coast. Maps were crude and many parts of the coast were uncharted. Navigation was mostly by 'dead reckoning' i.e. the shipmaster made a calculated guess as to how far, or in what direction his ship had travelled since he last fixed her position. But he could never be sure how much his ship had been pushed sideways by currents or wind.

During the summer of 1883 Alfred finally decided to take his son Charles out to New Zealand and to help him start a new life there as a joiner. Family letters confirm that Alfred himself was considering emigrating with his family if the 'Utopia' in New Zealand lived up to expectations.

On 28 August 1883 Alfred aged 40 years, Charles aged 18 years and Philip aged 12 years left Bollington. They would have travelled by train to London from the Waters Green Station, Macclesfield, opened in July 1873. At Gravesend they embarked on the sailing ship 'Lady Jocelyn' which was built for the General Screw Company in 1852. She was well known as an emigrant ship when Shaw Saville bought her in 1883.

Alfred and his sons would have been issued with Passengers Contract Tickets. This gives details of the fare in 1878 - £15.10s. for steerage accommodation, allowing 10 feet for luggage space and listing the victualling allowance per week and 1 gallon of water daily for all purposes.

In the Newspapers of 1870 - 1880's there were notices on the front page about Emigration.

MACCLESFIELD COURIER and HERALD

(Congleton Gazette, Stockport Express, Cheshire Advertiser)

2d unstamped 2½d stamped

EMIGRATION TO QUEENSLAND AUSTRALIA

SATURDAY, OCTOBER 2 1875

Free passages to Female Domestic Servants of good character

Wages in Colony £25 to £50 a year, all found

To Agricultural Labourers, married or single

Wages £30 - £50 a year with house and food

Assisted Passages to Mechanics, Artisans, Miners etc

On payment of £4.	Wages as under: -
Blacksmiths	10s to 12s a day
Carpenters	12s to 14s a day
Shoemaker	9s to 10s a day
Shipwrights	10s to 12s a day
Wheelwrights	10s to 12s a day
Miners, all kinds	10s to 12s a day

The above need not want work a single hour after landing
£20 land orders given to full paying passengers after 12 month's residence.
Handbooks sent post free on application to: -
Mr. F.Cooper, 20 Roe Street, Macclesfield (General Shipping Agent)

MACCLESFIELD COURIER and HERALD - JANUARY 1883
SHIPPING - REDUCED FARES TO AMERICA, CANADA AND AUSTRALIA
UNITED STATES £4 by FIRST CLASS STEAMERS
CANADA £3 & £4
QUEENSLAND £1 & £5
NEW SOUTH WALES £5
Secured Passages at once from:
F. COOPER
General Shipping Agent,
52 Roe Street,
MACCLESFIELD.

In January 1883 reduced fares were advertised. Were they also applicable to New Zealand? Alfred Wright decided to take Charles and Philip there and they sailed from London, 29 August 1883 on the Lady Jocelyn.

(Shaw Saville Records. Photostat Copy)
SHAW SAVILL & CO., 34 LEADENHALL STREET, LONDON
For THOMAS WARNOCK, BELFAST TO AUCKLAND. Fare £15.10.0. (Steerage) in respect of LADY JOCELYN, fifteenth May in 1878.

Steerage Passage had 10 Cubic Feet for Luggage per Adult, and victualled during the voyage (and any time of detention at any place before its termination) including Government Dues before embarkation and head money, if any, at the place of landing.

The following quantities, at least of Water and Provisions (to be issued daily) will be supplied by the Master of the Ship, as required by Law to each Statute Adult, Three Quarts of Water daily and a weekly Allowance of Provisions according to the following Scale:-

Scale of Dietary for each adult passenger per week

ARTICLES	SECOND CABIN	STEERAGE	ARTICLES	SECOND CABIN	STEERAGE
Preserved Meat	2 lb	1 lb	Coffee	3 oz	2 oz
Soup and Bouilli	$^1/_2$ lb	-	Butter	1 lb	6 oz
York Ham	1 lb	-	Cheese	$^1/_4$ lb	-
Fish	$^3/_4$ lb	-	Molasses	$^2/_3$ lb	$^1/_6$ lb
Indian Beef	$1^1/_2$ lb	$1^1/_2$ lb	Raisins or Currants	$^1/_2$ lb	$^1/_2$ lb
Mess Pork	$1^1/_2$ lb	$1^1/_2$ lb	Jams	$^1/_4$ lb	
Biscuit	$1^1/_4$ lb	$3^1/_2$ lb	Suel	6 oz	6 oz
Flour	$4^1/_4$ lb	3 lb	Pickles	1 pint	$^1/_2$ pint
Rice	1 lb	1 lb	Vinegar	$^1/_4$ pint	$^1/_3$ pint
Barley	$^1/_2$ lb	-	Mustard	$^1/_2$ oz	$^1/_2$ oz
Peas	$^2/_3$ pint	$^1/_3$ pint	Pepper	$^1/_4$ oz	$^1/_4$ oz
Preserved Milk	$^1/_4$ pint	-	Salt	3 oz	2 oz
Oatmeal	$^1/_3$ pint	1 pint	Potatoes (fresh) or	$3^1/_2$ lb	2 lb
Sugar – raw	1 lb	1 lb	Preserved ditto	$^1/_2$ lb	$^1/_2$ lb
Sugar – refined	4 lb	-	Water	2 Quarts	1 Quart
Tea	2 oz	2 oz	Lime Juice	?	?

Substitutes at the following rates may at the option of the Master be made in the above Dietary Scale

1 lb of Preserved Meat	for	1 lb Salt Pork or Beef
1 lb of Flour/bread/biscuit	for	$1^1/_2$ lb Oatmeal or
$^1/_2$ lb Beef or Pork	for	$1^1/_4$ lb Rice or Peas
1 lb Rice	for	$1^1/_2$ lb Oatmeal or vice versa
$^1/_4$ lb Preserved Potatoes	for	1 lb Potatoes
10 oz Currants	for	8 oz of Raisins
$2^1/_2$ oz Cocoa or Coffee	for	2 oz of tea
$^1/_3$ lb Treacle	for	$^1/_2$ lb Sugar
1 gill of Mixed Pickles	for	1 gill of Vinegar

NOTICE TO PASSENGERS

Deposit £7.15.0. Balance £7.15.0. to be paid at 31 Leadenhall Street, London, prior to embarkation. Total £15.10.0. It is understood that this Deposit will be absolutely forfeited in case the parties named fail to embark in a fit state of health for the voyage at the above mentioned date and place.

Passage to New Zealand

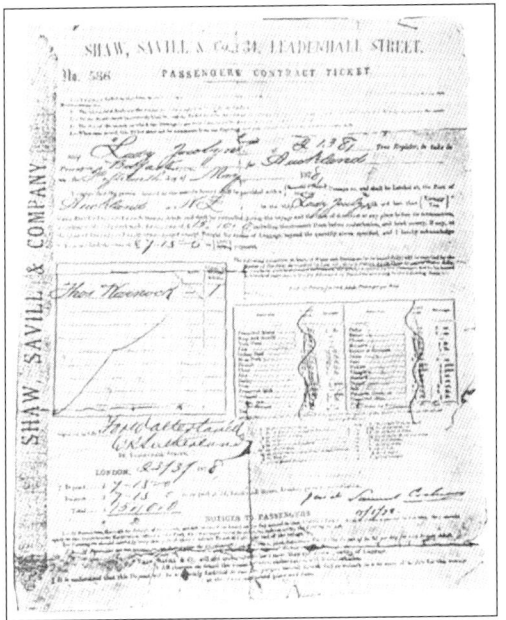

Passenger ticket for "Lady Jocelyn"

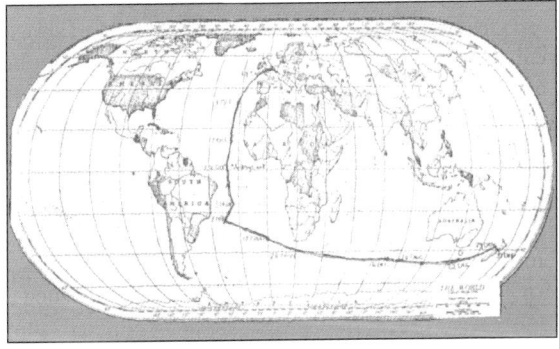

"Lady Jocelyn" in a storm in the English Channel, 2 September 1883. Sketch and poem sent by Alfred Wright to his family.

Route taken by the sailing ship "Lady Jocelyn" to take advantage of the trade winds. Plotted from the ship's log.

The voyage took 104 days.

Alfred and Philip Wright left New Zealand, as passengers on the steamship "Ruapehu", on 26 Sept. 1884. They arrived in London on 4 Jan. 1885, a voyage of 69 days.

'Lady Jocelyn' sailed from Gravesend on 30 August 1883 and cleared Deal a day later. There is a gap in Shaw Saville records concerning the events of the next 3 weeks. Family tradition and a picture of 'Lady Jocelyn' (sent by her father), which Martha Ann had framed with a poem underneath beginning 'Britannia, the pride of the ocean', said that there was a severe storm at sea and the ship was damaged. A local newspaper of 8 September 1883 confirms this in a long article about 'Incidents of the Storm'. There was loss of life and much damage to property and shipping all round the south and west coasts to the Bay of Biscay, and in particular the Channel, on Saturday and Sunday, 1st and 2nd of September.

From Shaw Saville records we know that 'Lady Jocelyn' sailed again from Portsmouth on 19 September 1883. So what repairs were completed there in 3 weeks? The Port Admiral, Portsmouth referred us to the Naval Historical Library, London who referred the query to the General Register and Record of Shipping and Seamen, Cardiff. Their records for the period are deposited at the P.R.O. in London.

Philip's son, Norman Wright, told us that in Portsmouth, the Wrights had stayed at "Aunt Aggies" - Agnes Weston Sailors Home - currently named the Royal Sailors Rest. (Their records were destroyed in the Blitz). The Portsmouth artist who recorded the 'Lady Jocelyn's' damaged rigging picture, delayed repairs while he sketched it.

Shaw Saville records confirm that:

> after 'Lady Jocelyn' left Portsmouth on 19 September 1883 she arrived in Wellington, New Zealand on 1 January 1884 after a 104 day voyage.

Life for the passengers must have been an interminable period of being crammed into crowded quarters - making little progress in calm weather and speeding along in the Trade Winds latitudes. In bad weather they had to be battened down for their own safety, sometimes for days on end. Food was barely adequate if travelling steerage. Our Alfred must have had a 'queasy tummy' as he mentions that he had diarrhoea for a month. Alfred's letter to John and Samuel tells of the sailors harpooning a shark. They ate the meat and carved the bones to make scrimshaw articles.

In New Zealand (from original letters home to his wife, Ann, dated February 1884) Alfred and his sons obtained lodgings with a widow, Mrs. Cotton, who lived in Lower Chapel Street, Auckland, North Island. They all obtained jobs quickly and had been working for a month when the letters were written. With difficulty, Alfred, Charles and Philip, had a studio photo taken to send home to England. However, Alfred's enteritis had recurred and he had been out of work for 8 days. Mill wages for joiners were 1/- to 1/6d a day, but self-employed joiners working outside earned 9/- to 10/- a day. Little skill was required for many jobs like erecting pre-fabricated wooden huts. There were too many immigrants and New Zealanders from South Island for the number of jobs available. Alfred visited Greg's friends and found them surprisingly poor. The 'Utopia' they had heard stories about was not to be found.

Alfred and Philip decided to return home to their family and Charles stayed in New Zealand. Alfred and Philip left him on Auckland Wharf on 15 September 1884 and they left Lyttleton on the evening of 26 September 1884 (4 days late) on board 'Ruapehu', one of the first steamships. She was one of 5 vessels ordered to establish the New Zealand Shipping Company's steam mail, passenger and cargo service between 1883-1898.

P&O have been most helpful in supplying details of 'Ruapehu's 'ship biography', her photograph and a print of a classic occasion on 14 February 1893 when she was overtaken by their sailing ship 'Turakina' in the 'Roaring Forties' - noted for its strong trade winds. 'Ruapeho' was a passenger/cargo liner built in 1883 by J.Elder & Co., Glasgow for the New Zealand Shipping Co. She was considered to be a handsome vessel, the barque rigged with clipper bows. There were 'handsome' facilities for 30 first-class passengers. However, fuel consumption was heavy and cargo capacity small - about 25,000 carcases of mutton.

There was a four weekly service from London to Auckland and Wellington, via Capetown and continuing round the world.

Alfred and Philip's return journey was made in better conditions than the previous one; no doubt costing more and completed in 9 weeks. They wrote home on the Channel, where their letter was put down with the rest of the mail and passengers at 8 am on Saturday 3 January 1885 at Plymouth. They hoped to arrive at Albert Dock, London on Sunday afternoon, 4 January, leave the boat on Monday and arrive in Bollington on Wednesday, 7 January. (Alfred's original letter gave the wrong date, actually 3 December 1884, later confirmed by the Lyttleton Times passenger list and Lloyd's Shipping list.)

In New Zealand, Charles married Leah Pattison, daughter of Joseph and Mary Pattison of Eden Terrace, Shaddock Street, Mount Eden. They were married by the chaplain at St.John's Church, Northcote and Charles' letter home announcing his marriage is dated 19 June 1886. They had one son, Alfred Hedley, b. 7 Dec.1888. There are photographs in the album of them all. Charles wrote letters to Aunt Mary Bennett and sister, Martha Ann.

During the 1914-18 war, Hedley served as a soldier in the New Zealand Engineers Expeditionary Force and was photographed in uniform. While serving in France, he sent embroidered postcards to his cousin, Mary Wright, and Martha Ann and Richard Wright's family. He came to England on one of his leaves, to stay with Aunt Martha Ann, Uncle Richard, with cousins Clifford, Mary and Leslie at Shrigley Road, Bollington, also Uncle Philip in Stockport. He told them his father Charles was a good cabinet maker joiner - when he was 'in work'. Evidently he couldn't hold down a job as he was an alcoholic. His wife Leah's letter confirms this.

There is a remarkable sequel to this emigration story. Enquiries to the National Library of New Zealand, Wellington, produced a photocopy of the "New Zealand Mail" for 4 January 1884 containing news of the newly berthed "Lady Jocelyn" with passenger and cargo lists (listing Alfred, Charles and Philip Wright.) It also included a detailed report from the ship's log supplied by the first mate, Mr.Codd. This records details of the storm in the English Channel, causing damaged rigging requiring repairs at Portsmouth, taking 3 weeks. The report gave the longitude and latitude bearings, from which its voyage has been roughly plotted on a map of the world. It shows that the sailing ship's route crossed the Atlantic towards South America to use the Trade Winds' power to sail to New Zealand. We sent copies of our original family letters to the Archives Section of the library, who had also sent copies of photographs of both the "Lady Jocelyn" and "Ruapehu" steamship.

Through contacting the New Zealand Family History Society, one of their members, Marie Corser, helped to trace Alfred Hedley Pattison Wright, only son of Charles and Leah (nee Pattison) Wright, who was still living in the family home, 33 Shaddock Street, Auckland. By using facts from our deposited copies of family letters, Marie obtained Charles and Leah's Marriage Certificate and Alfred Hedley's Birth Certificate, 7 Dec.1888. As Hedley had been a soldier in the New Zealand Expeditionary Force in 1914-1918 war, she obtained his army number 29540 and Regiment from National Archives and Service details from the Ministry of Defence Base Records. Hedley was an engineer fitter in the New Zealand Engineers. Marie found by searching Trade Directories for Auckland between 1940 to 1970's, that Alfred Hedley was listed still living in the family home.

FROM NEW ZEALAND MAIL,
4 January 1884
FROM LONDON

The Shaw, Savill and Albion Company's ship Lady Jocelyn, 2138 tons, Captain Watt, arrived off the Heads on Monday morning after a passage of 103 days from Plymouth, and was towed into port by the Stormbird, Tuesday, anchoring off the Queen's Wharf off 2 pm. We are indebted to her chief officer, Mr.Codd, for the following report of the passage from the ship's log.

"Left London on August 29th, and Gravesend next day at 2 pm., casting off the tug at Dungeness at 5.30 pm. Very fine weather with light airs and calms was experienced till September 1st, when a S.E. gale sprang up, veering round to S.S.W., and blowing very hard from that quarter. The ship was then between Portland Bill and Start Point. On the following day a heavy sea broke aboard, and damaged the ship to such an extent that it was considered advisable to return to port. On the morning of the 3rd, Portland Bill was sighted, and a course was shaped for Spithead, where she anchored at 10 am. On the 5th she was towed to Plymouth.

The necessary repairs having been effected, the ship proceeded to sea on September 18th in tow of a tug, which left her off the Isle of Wight at noon the same day. Had light and brisk breezes from ESE to SW, and passed Start Point at noon on the 19th. Thence had light variable winds, SW to NW with unsettled weather and occasional good runs to October 1st, when she got the NE Trades in lat. 33deg 11 min N and long. 20deg min W.

They were fresh with hazy weather, and were carried till October 7th in lat. 12 deg N and long 25 deg W. From this point had light and unsteady winds from S, SW and W, and then turning back to S till October 23rd, when a fresh southerly breeze was got. The equator was crossed on the 24th in long. 27 deg W 36 days out. The SE Trades were light, and well round to the southward, the vessel dragging the coast of South America in lat. 18 deg S, and long. 23 deg. Lost the Trades on November 2nd, getting calms and light variables till November when in lat. 23 deg S and long. 31 deg W got a steady breeze from N to NE, which lasted till the 13th. Thence to the meridian of Greenwich had the wind from all points of the compass with almost continuous rain. Crossed the meridian on the 15th, and that of the Cape of Good Hope on the 24th; reached long. 90 deg 37 min E on Dec 6th, crossed the meridian of the Leeuwin on the 14th, ln lat. 47 deg 23 min S, and rounded Tasmania on the 22nd. The casting was made between the parallels of 43 and 48 degs. Had light but steady winds from S round by the westward to N till Dec 6th, thence SE and NE to the 13th, and brisk and moderate winds from NW to W and SW to Tasmania. Had variable winds with rain thence till the 28th, when a heavy SE gale was experienced. Made Cape Farewell on the morning of the 29th, and was becalmed the whole day. Had light SE winds from the 30th till making the Heads at 6 am. on the 31st, when a fresh NW breeze sprang up. Was boarded by Pilot Holmes at 5.30 pm, stood off and on during the night, and was towed in as above."

As on the occasion of her previous visit, the Lady Jocelyn comes into port in a scrupulously clean condition. She brings a number of first, second, and third class passengers. A commercial traveller named Robert Williams, in the second cabin, died during the passage of melancholy. Every effort was made to rouse him from the listlessness into which he had fallen, but they produced not the slightest effect. He is understood to have left a wife and family in the west of England. Two births also occurred. The general health of the passengers was good. The vessel is in command of Captain Watt, well known in the colony as commander of the ship Wanganui. The chief officer is Mr. Codd, formerly occupying a similar position on the last named vessel. These gentlemen, together with Dr. Cree and the other officers of the ship, were yesterday morning presented with the following flattering testimonial:-

> "We, the undersigned passengers of the Lady Jocelyn, in sincerely thanking Captain Watt for his care and attention during the passage from London, desire to express our appreciation of the thorough seamanlike qualities displayed by him, particularly during the adverse circumstances attending the commencement of the voyage, and of his unremitting solicitude for the safety of the ship and passengers at all times. We also desire to thank the first and second officers, Messrs Codd and Walker, for the able manner in which they have carried out Captain Watt's orders, and for their extreme courtesy during the passage. We have also to acknowledge our indebtedness to Dr. Cree, the surgeon of the ship, for the skilful way in which he has discharged his onerous duties, and for his kind attention generally.
> Signed by the first and second class passengers."

The Lady Jocelyn hauled into No. 2 berth at the Queen's Wharf on Wednesday morning, and broke bulk immediately.

PASSENGER LIST OF LADY JOCELYN. LONDON TO WELLINGTON. AUGUST 1883 - JAN 1884

From New Zealand Mail 4 Jan 1884. Uncertain names are marked with ?
LADY JOCELYN, ship, 2138 tons, Watt (i.e. Captain Watt) from London and Plymouth.

Saloon Passengers:
Herbert G Wilson, Herbert T Dickane?, Miss E Barnard, Miss M Bodger? Neville and Gordon Shute, Lowton and Mrs.Lowton, William, Ada L and Catherine Bates, Herbert J Dixie, R Farrant, W R Scott, Hugh Fraser, G A Kemperman, Miss M Moorshed, L.E.M Corbett, James and Arthur Broonhead, Mr H and Mrs Wrigley.

Second cabin:
Charles L Spencer, Smith, Wylie, Thomas? Cranewick, George M and Elizabeth Marriott, John W Newman, Miss Harriet Furniss, Henry James Flint, Robert and Mrs.Manton, William (2) Edith (2) Florence and John Brown, Andrew Johnston, Annie Hallahan, R. Williams, W.H.Dixon.

Steerage:
John, Margaret and Dorothy Parves; Edgar J Davies, W.H.Gilbertson, Rebecca Coleman, Charles C, Frank R, and Albert P. Blades, Joseph, Ann, Frank, Harry, Annie, Alfred and Rosamund Loasby?: Thomas, Emily, Rose, William, Elizabeth and Albert Dretton; Lucy, Frank, Arthur and Carrie Hockley; Richard and Ruth White; W.Downward, Sarah Burton or Dutton, Henry Kent; Seth, Mary A and Clara Blachard; William Esther, John, Annie, Henry, Mary, Catherine, William, Herbert and Thomas Willis; Elizabeth George and Edward B Osborne; Joseph E., Mrs. Alfred J.C., Robert C, Elsie D., George W., Percy F., Mary E., Alice M., Dorothy E., and Harold D. Cobb; Robert G.N. Susannah, Robert, Alice J and Florence Parker; Fanny Dure?, Annie M., Phillip S., and Annie Andrew; Wm.N.Probyn, Henry Neak, Henry Hughs, William and Ann Allan, Robert E Shine, Charles R.Clay, P.King, James O.Lawrence; **Alfred, Charles and Phillip Wright;** Teresa Reverald, Joseph Hall, Robert Alderney, Ernest Collier, Caroline Cowling, Levin and Co. Agents

A commercial traveller named Robt.Williams, in the second cabin, died during the passage of melancholy. He is understood to have left a wife and family in the west of England.
Two births also occurred.

The vessel is in command of Captain Watt, well known in the colony as commander of the Ship Wanganui. His chief officer is Mr. Codd, formerly occupying a similar position on the last-named vessel. From 1st mate's report of the voyage, second officer is Mr. Walker and Surgeon of the ship is Dr. Cree.

FROM THE LYTTLETON TIMES 27 NOVEMBER 1884. P4.

SAILED - Nov. 26 RUAPEHU (ss 2655 tons)

Brough for Plymouth, via Rio Janeiro, New Zealand Shipping Company, agents.

Saloon Passengers:-

Mr & Mrs Alex.Matheson, Mr & Mrs Francis, Mr.D.S.Neave, Misses Adelaide, Constance and Alice Mary Neave, Mr & Mrs Frederick C.Halketh, Miss Georgina C.Glover, Mr.M.Smith.

Second Saloon:-

Mr & Mrs. Edwin L.Millett, Mary & Richard Millett, Mr.Charles Woodford, Mr.Carroll Andsell, Misses Emily Peach and Christina Lennox, Messrs. Arthur Levy, J.W.Wepstead, Captain Bayldon? Mrs. Johanna Everleigh, Miss Jane M. Seymour, Edward Speechley, David Brodie and John Barclay.

Steerage:-

Mrs. Mary Ballantyne and child, Mrs. Mary Ann Brown and child, Messrs. **Alfred and Philip Wright,** John Edwards, Charles White, G.Bassenelli, C.J.Riley, H.Ravencroft, Walter Duckett, Mr. & Mrs. George Holder, Misses Harriet, Mary, Emily, Gertrude, Masters George and Harold Holder, Miss Alice Louisa Field, Mr. & Mrs. Richard Willock, Misses Lister Willock, Elizabeth Willock, and Annie Willock, Masters Frank Willock and George Willock, Mrs Augustus Skinner and family (3), F Stahlschmidt, L.Bartoli, A.H.Riley, J Lennox, T.J.Burnett, Wm. Hodgkinson, T.Tobin, M.Fawcett.

Trooper in Cheshire Yeomanry uniform
Photograph of unidentified family member, about 1853/4, Crimean War. Taken from the original glass plate deposited at the Cheshire Record Office, 1977 who made the negative and print for family records.

Alfred Hedley Wright
Engineers Fitter in the New Zealand Engineers, wearing the uniform of the New Zealand Expeditionary Force in the First World War
(1914 – 1918)

The electoral roll of 1975 confirmed that he was still at the same address. Marie then wrote to Hedley asking if he was the same person we were trying to find. He replied that he was, in a firm hand for 88 years. Eric Bandelow, Hedley's adopted son, replied on his behalf. On receiving this exciting news, we wrote a welcoming letter to Hedley, enclosing two newspaper articles about his Aunt Martha Ann Wright and her eldest son, his cousin, Clifford, (b.8 Dec.1897 d. 11 May 1986). One reported how Martha Ann celebrated her 100th Birthday on 1 Sept 1968, the second told of Clifford, widowed, making marmalade and selling it for Bollington Methodist Church funds. Eric's second letter enclosed a photograph of Hedley in his 80s. The family resemblance to his cousin, Clifford, was remarkable (especially the nose). Eric later wrote to tell us of Hedley's death on 1 Nov. 1982 aged 94 years. Sadly, Eric and Iris answered no further letters after Christmas 1984.

8

Letters From New Zealand

From Alfred Wright

Lower Chapel St

Auckland

Sunday afternoon - Feb 17 1884

My very dear Wife,

I write you to say that we are all of us well in health at present, though since I wrote my father a fortnight ago I have again been troubled with diarrhoea, which is very weakening, but I am all right now. I do not know what causes it. I was not troubled with it at home more than a day or two at a time. But on the ship I had it a month and this time a fortnight. Since I wrote my father I have been idle 8 days but expect to be at work some time this next week. At the building I was working at the plasterers were in our way so about 14 of us were stopped last Friday week. Unlike the builders at home none of the builders here have any workshop or yard and men are simply engaged at the building that is in the course of erection to fix the prepared work from the sash and door factories. And everything in the way of prepared work is done at the factories by machinery as much as it possibly can be. And this as you see caused a deal of changing and loss of time to carpenters who work outside the mills. The wages in the mills for joiners are a 1/- or 1/6 per day less than those have who work outside. The outside wage is 9/- and 10/- per day. I expect to have 10/- from this next week. Philip and Charles have had no idle time yet, and I hope they may not have. They have been at work a month now. Things in the south island are very bad now, and the government here have been paying the passage up from Christchurch of all who cared to come, and then with so many immigrants arriving here from the old country (or home as it is always called) Auckland is quite flooded with labour of all sorts.

I think Charles Rimmer's plan is the best here, to do work on one's own account as he did when here and if one could only begin and have work, the lads would be a little fortune to one, but of course this requires caution and money, though caution is the principal thing. I see nothing in the erection of framed houses that I and the lads could not manage well enough, and so be our own masters, if we could only begin Long credit is given to builders at the factories where the timber is obtained for work, though there would be some caution used by them to strangers like myself for a time. I have no complaint to make of the lads, they are both good, and work hard. I am specially pleased with Charles, he is both sober and industrious and seems wishful to get on. He does not altogether approve of lying on the floor with Philip and thinks it would be advisable to get a small iron bed each as soon as we can afford. We have an empty bedroom and the use of the kitchen for 6/- per week and this is considered very cheap here.. The house is an old one but is in the centre of the city so that we are right for work in any direction. The old lady (a widow) earns every week £3 by doing washing for ship's officers herself alone, and says she has many a time for weeks running earned a pound a day, and does still when she has a woman to help her. She does nothing under 4/- per doz, and the officers clothes have not any dirt upon them scarcely. Since we left home Charles and I have done our own washing up to this last week, but this last wash our landlady is favouring us by doing it at 2/- per doz. We have had the starch washed out of our collars and have put them away clean and now we are wearing paper ones which we obtain at from 3d to 9d per doz. The curse of our travelling has been the luggage. Oh the nuisance it has been.

When I arrived at Wellington from the ship I immediately sent enquiring letters to the Atkinsons at Nelson in the S.Island and also to Mrs.D.Atkinson at Kamo, in the province of Auckland in the North Island, to know what the prospects of constant employment in their locality might be. Their replies I enclose. But before I got answers I had decided to come to the city of Auckland here. So I took a steamer that called at Nelson. Nelson I found to be a pretty place and country, though quiet. The Atkinsons there I found were very well spoken of and are also very well to do. They are lawyers. I did not go to them as I was not going to stay there, but simply to see the place.

This last week having time on my hands I decided to go to Kamo Wangerie 90 miles north of Auckland. I found upon my arrival there all your suppositions as to Mrs.D.Atkinson being in poor circumstances to be quite true. They live in an house that I should be sorry to put you in, nor do I think there are many working men in N.Z. worse off, and yet you will see by the way she wrote to me she still retains her grand conventional high class notions. I thought her very much wanting in common hospitality. Poverty is no disgrace if it be honest poverty, but I did not at all like the way I was entertained which was not owing to her poor circumstances. But this you must keep to yourself or else there will be a mistake made if it should be known. With respect to what she says about carpenters being fully employed it was I found all nonsense, certainly they are fully employed but then it is with their fruit farms when there is nothing else to be done, and I could see it was useless for me and the lads to go there expecting to have constant employment at our trade.

It is pretty country and oranges and grapes grow to great perfection. There is also a great coal mining business carried on there. The quantity of coal there so far as is known is unlimited, it is 10/- per ton! here it is 27/- per ton at Wellington it was 37/- and £2 per ton.

Mr.D.Atkinson is engaged in a little way in making Portland cement. Time back he told me he had been unfortunate in land speculations.

I am trying to get into the government railway carriage works and he said he thought he could be of service to me as he is acquainted with the manager here.

Please give my best love to my very dear daughter, she knows all that I want of her. You may tell her and Miss Dunnington that I notice the girls and ladies here to be not a bit behind their sisters at home in dress and fashions Please give my love to father and mother, to Aunt Mary, to Aunt Grace, to Miss Dunnington and to all you know I regard and esteem. Philip and Charles also send their best love to you all.

My present address is
Care of Mrs.Cotton
Lower Chapel St.
Auckland, N.Z.

But I think it would be best for you to direct your letters to the Chief Post Office, Auckland, as I allways know when the mails arrive, and my place of residence is uncertain.
Charles wants the letters to be sent to the first address as Mrs.Cotton will take charge of them in any case. So please direct them to the house. And now with my best love to you my dear wife and sons.
I remain
Your affectionate husband and father
Alfred Wright

Please write to me as soon as you can. I am anxious to know something about you.
Please do not exhibit my letters to you to anyone. I never received any reply from Jim Reeves at Christchurch. Mr. Kimball told me when at Wellington that he was a very great rogue, he knew him well, and up to a few years ago had a good business and property too, but drink had beggared both him and his wife together with roguishness and he is now working as a poor carpenter.

Auckland, N.Z.
April 28 1884

My very dear Sons, John and Samuel,

I must to begin with ask to be excused for not putting this letter in an envelope of its own but as I had none that would just fit it and not being near a shop to buy one, and knowing that it would be quite safe in grandfathers envelope I thought it would not matter so much.

I must now tell you that when on the ship coming to New Zealand where both the air and the sea were warm, a number of pretty little birds, green and yellow, used to come and alight on the rigging. Their bills were hooked like a parrotts, but they were too wide awake to be caught.

We saw too most of the way a number of different sorts of sea birds, some very large. One morning in an hours time when the sea was as smooth as glass 20 large albatrosses were caught with hook and line, and from the tip of one wing to the tip of the other they measured 10 or 12 ft. Hedley will show you on the floor how much this is. The sailors took the long fine bones out of their wings to make pipes of for smoking and their large thick beautiful breasts of white down were cured for ladies muffs. Mother Careys chickens were the most numerous but the Cape pigeon was the prettiest of them all.

We saw too a great many porpoises: fish about 4 or 5 ft long with long noses like Irish pigs but these were only seen when the water was rough. We saw too a many flying fish, these are about the size of an herring with long furry wings that enable them to fly quickly over the water when the dolphins are chasing them. One morning a dolphin was harpooned and when it was cut open there was a flying fish inside it, I suppose that it had just caught for breakfast.

But I must now tell you of the sharks that came about the ship. One day the sailors threw a harpoon at one but the shaft only struck its side, but you should have seen how angrily it returned to the ship to give battle to some thing. Then a shark hook was thrown out with a piece of salt beef on it. The hook was fastened to a chain so that the shark might not bite the hook off, and the chain to a line which we held in our hands. The shark soon took the beef in its mouth, but it did not know of the hook but it soon found out what a mistake it had made when we began hauling at the line. It did splash and kick about I can tell you. When it was close up to the ship a rope was slipped down the line with a noose over its head and then drawn tightly round its tail. Then another was run down over its head and drawn tight behind its gills. After this we pulled him up on to the ship and though its mouth was torn and bleeding from the hook, it bit a thick rope in two as easily as Martha Ann snaps her thread with her teeth. Then when it was quite secure one of the sailors drove a knife into its head but even with this I should think it was quite an hour in dying. After it was dead it was cut open and its back bone taken out to make one of the gentlemen a walking stick, and a nice stick it made too. Sailors you must know are very clever at making all sorts of nice things, things that would quite surprise you if you were to see them.

We saw too many whales but these were generally a distance from the ship. When we were at Wellington 3 whales got into the harbour and when they were seen by the boatmen they were driven to where the water was shallow and when the tide went away they were left helpless aground. The boatmen then got to them in their boats and battered them on the head with oars until they were dead, but before this they had been harpooned and made fast by the ropes being tied to logs of the railway. I was told the boatmen got £80 for them for boiling down for oil.

We saw too what is called a squall, but this is neither a bird or a fish, but a wind that blows very suddenly and sometimes does great mischief to a ship if the sails are not quickly taken in. But our sailors ran up the rigging like squirrels and quickly had us tight for a good blow, and blow it is I assure you. We can see it come rolling over the still water like a cloud and then it whistles and hisses through the ropes, but is soon over. And it makes one think of the great God that rules everything and of his wonderful works to see the great waves heaving and rolling as it they meant to drown us all; but we asked God to take care of us and we trusted in him and felt no fear because it is as easy for him to bring death to us on land as on water, and we knew too that our ship was a good one and merrily she rode the waves big as they were.

I think I ought to tell you of the beautiful sunsets on the water but it would be altogether impossible for me to describe them. There is every variety of colour and these showing against the clouds and on the water make such a picture that to say the least is grand, very grand. And here in N.Z. we have very fine sunsets and such fine sunny clear weather that it makes one almost inclined to stand still on the road and thank God for it. And now in conclusion I must thank you for writing to us, we are glad you have not forgotten us. I think Samuels letter capital, especially the last verse of his song. I was so pleased to read it. I hope both of you will be all that it says and to be so I think it would be best to begin by helping mother all you possibly can and I feel sure this is the very best way to become great men, especially if your conduct is altogether good, good at school, and good at chapel and good everywhere. I cannot tell you how much I want you to be good, and honest and truthful, and now I must say good bye and good night for it is quite bedtime.

From your loving and afft.father.

Alfred Wright

My dear Daughter,

In the first place I must acknowledge the receipt of mother's reply to the letter I sent Grandfather. I was glad to learn that Grandmother is so far recovered as to be able to go about again, but I am very sorry that Grandfathers illness is so protracted. I trust that the next news we have from home will be that he is fully restored.

It is with pleasure that I learn that you have been attentive to them in their distress. This was your duty but I can quite believe that you have been actuated by better and kindlier motives. I thank you very much for this and shall try to remember you in a more substantial way by and by.

I am very thankful too to know that you all keep in satisfactory health and that you are getting along tolerably well. Will you please tell Mrs.Orme I thank her for the card. I quite expected what it has come to, but how gratifying to know he had made preparation for the worst. And so may we be wise in time. I sincerely trust that you and I may not suffer the thoughts for the welfare of our never dying souls to be smothered with the concerns of this life. Little as we regard this matter nothing can possibly be of such importance to us as deciding at once for Christ, we cannot tell how soon the call may be for us and if when it comes what a mistake we shall have made if not ready to answer it. And then how comforting to know that Jesus is our friend, always sympathising with us and ever ready to help us in our troubles; and how ungrateful of us after he has done and suffered so much, all for our happiness, to disregard his love and pain him with wrong doing, and by keeping him out of our hearts. I do not want to preach to you, but I do want you to become a Christian; it is the only way to be really happy and you cannot be safe without.

I enclose a letter which was awaiting my arrival at Wellington from one of the young ladies at Portsmouth. I send it to you because I want you to be my confidential to keep it for me. The young lady is just what I should like you to be kind and good.
And I noticed too that not only the writer of the letter but the other young ladies with her were very plainly and neatly dressed, though very wealthy and of high position. It seemed to have been their care to avoid 'panniers' and the rest of the foolish nonsense that hangs about a ladies dress now-a-days, and I assure you that their plain close fitting dresses set off their tall handsome persons finely and to the best advantage.

I felt a little annoyed that the letters I had written for home reading should have been sent out for the perusal of others. This is a course I do not approve of as we do not know who we are writing for, therefore I ask you to do me the favour to keep this letter to your self.

During the past month I have kept well but a fortnight ago Charles came home ill on the Saturday, he looked very ill and it had been quite as much as he could do to get home, he was feverish but a good sweating in bed rendered him able to go to work on the Monday.

Philip I have taken from the brush works, he made his clothes so very dirty and have placed him in the N.Z. sash and door factory, he has 9/- per wk to begin with for 47 hrs. A week or so ago another lad carelessly threw a piece of wood which struck Philip on the head and though he had Walters R.N. cap on it cut through to the bone and bled very much. When he came home I washed the place and cut the hair away and then plastered it up and it is now allmost well. On friday he had the ill luck to get his thumb trapped with a piece of wood over the nail, it has pained him a good deal, but as saturday was the Queen's birthday he had a rest and I think he will be able to go again in the morning.

Last Sunday but one Philip and I went again on Mt. Eden, it was a charming day and the air so clear, we could see a very long distance. The land across from sea to sea is only 7 miles, and when we were on the top the waters seemed very near.

There is a fine landscape to view from the top and to see the homesteads dotted here and there over the country seemed very pretty. Mt. Eden is the largest of the volcanoes about here, and though it is many hundreds of ft. above the sea it must at one time have been level with it, as the earth even up to the crater is full of sea shells, but all the country here has in some past age been all of a boil.

We thank you for the papers you have sent us, but do not send us any more "Tit Bits" unless you send them under the book rate of postage as they are not registered as newspapers for transmission abroad. We had to pay 11d for the packet you sent us, deficient postage and fine, and for the letter 6d deficient postage and 6d fine. All your letters have been over weight, but we do not mind paying deficient postage, but the fine would be saved if you stamped them correctly. 6d stamp for every $1/2$ oz. Tit Bits we are glad of but stamp them under the book rate please.

The weather is now very chilly and cold nights and mornings, and we have had much rain lately but I suppose we must be reminded by this that it is now winter time.

I am sorry we are not able to send you the photographs this mail, but the fault is not ours (except that we have delayed the business so long) we have been twice to be taken but they were failures each time owing to our not being able to get there soon enough on the Saturday before the light loses its strength, and now we shall have to lose time in the day to be taken. One or two Saturdays when we could have been there in time it has been raining, so you see it has been quite an humbugging business. We are disgusted with it.

Philip takes great interest in shipping matters, he knows every boat and her business belonging to the port of Auckland. I quite regard him as an authority upon shipping matters. We still have a many fires here, though not so many I think as when first we came; some of them are rather serious ones, and you would be surprised with what rapidity framed houses are consumed when the fire has once fastened upon them. The heat is very great. But they are all good for carpenters though I never like to be wakened up in the stillness of night by the clang of the fire bells. Some of the wooden boarding houses are very large with a many rooms in them, and if any of these were to take fire I do not see how those in the upper stories could get down. Philip thinks it would never do for mother to live in a house above the ground floor as in that case she could tumble through any of the windows outside on to the ground without injury.

Philip wishes me to ask you to thank Aunt Mary for the pin, he likes it very much and says he shall take care of it. He wishes to be kindly remembered to you and thinks if his thumb had not been sore he should have written to either Grandmother or Samuel. He has bought a war cry for Aunt Grace, it is enclosed in the newspaper.

Eggs are now 2/9 per doz., last week we were asked 3/- but we do not buy them at this price, though in consequence our rice and corn flour puddings have to suffer for it. We have a quart of new milk per day at 4d per qt but it is very rich and good and I dare not tell you how many chops and beef steaks we speculate in, but these are very cheap.

Tell John there are a many goats kept about Auckland, some of them are pretty little things, some boys seem to keep them as pets.

This morning being rather bright we decided to go again to the photographers at noon. We went but as the day has been cloudy I cannot say they will be good ones. To compensate you for this delay when we do send our photos we will send you one or two of the maoris. They are a fine people but the women as a rule cannot compare to the men. When Tawhiao the king was leaving his hotel here for England he was told that he might not by any means walk down to the ship, so a cab was called, but he positively refused to get inside, he said a seat on the box was more befitting a king, so away to the ship by the side of the driver he went.

There is in one of the shop windows here two fine paintings of a maori and his wife. The price of them is £100.

In the museum here there are a many things belonging to the natives some wonderful carvings, canoes, spears, greenstone weapons and there is one hatchet much worn with which one of the chiefs killed his victims. Up to a few years ago they were canibals; there are also some very tastefully and curiously made mats which are for wear on the person, very pretty.

Mother wishes to know what has become of the Yorkshire farmer. He is at present 150 miles north of this place farming for a gentleman named Graham. He is about nominating his family for N.Z. but I will tell her more when I write her.

There is a great amount of work going on here of different kinds. There are several large and costly buildings in the course of erection, besides smaller fry, but as I have stated in previous letters there are a great many people to do the work, too many. This is the only place in all N.Z. at present in a flourishing state, and from every where else in the colony people have been flocking here. A many people from Sydney have come here owing to the slackness of things there. To say nothing of the new chums from the old Country, indeed it is a puzzler to me what becomes of them all or how they all manage to live.

I enclose P.O.O. for £5, four of which if mother approves, I desire to be given to Aunt Mary in consideration of the dear little lad who is sleeping his long sleep there. The remaining one is to make my promise good with Hedley. I do not suppose his fiddling will bring him much bread and cheese, but music is good for enlivening the spirit and is a fine accomplishment, therefore I wish him success in acquiring the knowledge of it. I am highly pleased that you are making such fine progress.
Please give my best love to Mother, Grandmother and Grandfather to Aunt Mary and every body I care for especially to Hedley John and Samuel and believe me to be my dear very dear daughter.
Your affectionate Father
Alfred Wright
Please do not forget what I ask of you in the beginning part of my letter.

Auckland, N.Z.
Sunday morning;- July 20th 1884

My dear Sister,

We send you this letter in the hope that you are in good health and enjoying the fine summer weather Ann spoke of in her last despatch (May 7). I have been very sorry to learn by home letters that you have not enjoyed unbroken good health since I last saw you; but I suppose we are to have occasional reminders of our frailty. I am very thankful to know that at home the bill of health is kept tolerably clean and for ourselves I am also thankful to add that we keep well and hearty with good appetite.

With us it is the worst part of winter for the last 3 weeks we have had almost incessant rain, day and night, showers the likes of which you seldom see at home, making it very bad for outdoor work and rendering the roads and streets terrible with mud; but for winter time it is very warm, no frost, and the sun comes out with great power; the days too are stretching now.

By the last mails we sent home the photos of our precious selves and a few Maoris, but I am sure they will come to grief before arriving as we neglected tying twine round the envelopes and as they were very heavy I am sure they will burst the envelopes. I hope Ann will tell us know she received them, for they were an awful lot of trouble to us, setting aside the cost.

Ann wishes us very much to return but she does not wish this more than I wish to see her, the best of wives. As regards returning to Bollington I have somewhat a dread of it, as I feel certain it will be hard lines to make a living there, and the miserable thoughts of the leasing transaction still haunts me when I think about it. But I feel it would be cruelty to urge her to come out as her feelings and inclinations are; so I have made up my mind to return home before the winter at home begins, I and Philip. Charles prefers to stay, and indeed it is by far the best for him to remain. Philip does not want to return but I could not think of leaving him here with Charles. And I expect the next winter will tell seriously against my father, considering the hard time he had last. I shall be sorry to leave the place for I have got to like it very much.

For the past fortnight Charles and I have not done so well as hitherto, as I have said the weather is exceedingly wet and we are too in the thick of a general election and these things tell rather against prosperity. I am sorry to add too that there are scores, nay hundreds out of employment. With this place being in a thriving state and the rest of the Colonies depressed every boat coming from the south and from Australia has brought people here in the hope of doing better, so that the place is quite overdone with workers. There is plenty of work to be done but there are far too many people to do it. For the past month we have had two young men up from Wellington, living with us, that were fellow passengers on the L.Jocelyn. They have done exceedingly badly since arriving in N.Z. I am very sorry for this as they are two good fellows especially Robert Alderney, and whilst this wet weather lasts and the turmoil of the elections continues doing well is out of the question.

I am so glad to learn that my daughter is doing so well on the piano thus showing we have some talent in the family. I doubt Hedley will not be so persevering with his violin. I hope I am mistaken as the fiddle and piano go well together and music is a grand accomplishment. I wish you and they could be at the services here in the Theatre, you would be greatly entertained. Sankey's hymns are sung by a most excellent choir and nothing in the way of music would please me better than to hear these nice tunes performed by my own son and daughter. Philip is quite prepared to sing whilst they play.

Perhaps you would be wishful to know more particularly of Charles here. I am glad to say he has not I believe tasted drink since coming here, thus improving his habits some though he still continues the loathsome use of tobacco, his evenings when fit to go out are generally spent in the public reading room with an occasional attendance at the services at the Y.M.C.A. rooms. Philip generally stays in the evenings he does not care much to go out in the dark, though sometimes he finds his way to the market to see the rabbits and fancy birds there on sale, but oftener he goes to see the shipping as he is immensely taken up with this. This last week he has spoiled the peace of the house making a bird cage, as he wants to have one of these many coloured birds as his own.

If you want to know anything of fashion and dress here I may say that it is chiefly of the American stamp indeed almost everything is American. The fair sex as at home are very dressy, and appear to like showing themselves off. They are also the greatest sinners in intemperance. It is rather an unusual thing to see a man intoxicated, but not so women.

This I account for that as the wooden houses are generally small which are the homes of working men there is little to do in the way of house work and as the husband gets as a rule large wages the good wife has plenty of time to spend the money and this I think she often does, here. The dress too of the men is after the American style. If you saw the young dandies as they turn out with their bell legged pants and fine white shirts showing full and wide down to the bottom waistcoat button, fancy narrow tie, broad slouched hat, and cigar I think you would be inclined to laugh. But loose as some people assert this place to be, I believe it bears no comparison to Melbourne for gaiety and fun and loose living.

You would be surprised at the number of Scotch people here, one hears the Scotch tongue on every side, and here too as at home they aspire to the best positions. There are also a many Londoners here and their way of speaking is the prevailing one. The people here are as a rule very polite and respectful but seem rather cold hearted and distant. I am not taken up with those I have had to do with. I like the country much better than I like the people.

In conclusion I ask you to give my best love to my dear wife the next time you see them, and to my daughters and sons. Tell Samuel I am sorry that he is a naughty boy and giving his mother trouble, and ask Ann to kindly remember me to my father and mother and to Aunt Grace. We send our best respects too to Aunt Phebe and believe me to be

Your afft. brother in law
Alfred Wright

'Ruapehu' English Channel
Saturday Morn. *Dec 3 1885
*Actually January 3 1885

My dear Wife

I take this opportunity to inform you that we are so far safe and sound after an excellent voyage for speed and weather.

We did not leave Lyttleton until the evening of the 26 November 4 days later than the advertised time consequently we are somewhat late here. This delay caused us to have nearly a week to wait at Lyttleton but we went to Christchurch and spent the time there.

We left Charles at the Auckland Wharf on Saturday Nov 15 well and hearty, he was working over, so he could not stay to see us off.

We shall arrive at Plymouth about 8 o'clock this morning to deliver passengers and mails, and we expect to be in Albert Dock, London on Sunday afternoon but we shall not leave the ship until Monday morning, at least so we are told. I think you may expect us with you on Wednesday, possibly on Tuesday but I think not.

I remain
Your afft.husband
Alfred Wright

Excuse the writing please for the vibrations of the screw make writing almost an impossibility. We wish you all a happy New Year.

P.S. If we find the weather very bad in London we shall come home at once.

7.30 a.m. We are now anchored in Plymouth Harbour. It is raining fast.

---

* Alfred Wright should have dated his letter January 3 1885, which makes sense of the Happy New Year part.
From Lloyd's Weekly Shipping Index 1884 & 1885 Ruapehu's voyage and dates check with these - sailing from Lyttleton 26 Nov 1884 arriving London 4 Jan 1885 (a Sunday according to Cheyney's Handbook of Dates) a journey of 40 days (and not 8 days 26 Nov - 3 Dec!)

From Charles Wright

Cambridge St. Auc. N.Z.
Sunday April 27/84

Dear Sister

I am glad to hear you are all well and have escaped the complaints going about the neighbourhood. It is Sunday and a beautiful day too, for the beginning of Winter. To me it is like a splendid English summer day but the old Colonials think it cool, especially in the mornings when they go wrapped up to their work at 8 o'clock saying it is hard work to get up so early these cold mornings. To say the truth I like this beautiful land better than the Old Country. We have had a good deal of roughing it especially at first though we are doing well now. If I were to go into every particular since we landed it would take me a week to relate with my slow writing. Now in writing to you remember I am not writing to Gregs, anything like showing such meddlesome gentry our letters I never heard of. I could spin them a yarn about their very hospitable and awfully rich relations here that would not be such a "pleasure" for them to read.

My chief object in writing to you is to impress on you all the many advantages to be gained by coming. The climate and scenery and everything relating to the land has never been overrated nor can it be. There is no doubt but that it is the finest in the world. The wages are good, provisions are cheap and plentiful and there is no doubt but that if Mother was managing for us that she would keep us all on the same amount of money that it takes to keep us three. There is such a scarcity of female servants that notwithstanding the shiploads coming in almost every week that girls are engaged at enormous wages both in town and country. The Colonial girls are much to proud to go out to work and as for dress and fashion they are before their English sisters both in taste and beauty.

I am working at 24s per week but I shall not work at my next job for less than 2£. I have lost but 2 days out of the many holidays Easter Monday and Anniversary Day.

Now if you will do your best to get mother and Aunt Mary to come we will get land and before very long have a handsome villa residence furnished and ready for you to take possession. The house we can build ourselves and for excellence of design and finish can not be beat by the Governors itself. But of course to do this we shall have to keep our 10£ a month here (that is the amount we can easily save) I am glad to say that my present wage pretty near keeps us, houserent cat and all. Now what more can I say we do not as the Wesleyans at home say "Come over and help us" but come over and with us enjoy the benefits of this glorious land. It is not for myself that I desire you to come, your coming will have no very particular benefit to me but with the many advantages to be gained, to yourselves, the inferiour state of fathers health, and good society, and fathers great wish to settle in this sunny land I think the idea is well worthy of consideration.

What is there at home to stop for. I never even dream of going back to settle. I might take a trip to see the miserable old place again but going back for good is not to be thought of.

I will tell you the way to come do not on any account come by the Shaw Saville and Albion Co. boats nor indeed by any sailing ship at all. First let us know and we will nominate you by that means you can come for next to nothing. The secure a passage in the N.Z. Shipping Cos. splendid line of Mail Steamers or by the Peninsular and Oriental Steamship Cos. to Melbourne and Sidney and then across to Auckland by the Union Steam Ship Cos. splendid line of steamers. By paying a little more money yourself Mother and Aunt Mary could come 2nd Cabin and the boys 3rd where they would do very well with you to look after them a bit.

I must thank you for sending me such a nice letter.

Tell Grandfather and Grandmother I am very sorry to hear of their severe illness but they will soon be better now this warm weather has come.

It did take me a time to gain my land legs after being so long aboard ship sometimes when I would go round a corner the building would suddenly lean over and give me a smack on the side of the head which would make me stand sermonise for some minutes. The people here have a very nice and correct way of pronouncing their words which very soon made me be noticed, sometimes they would ask me what county I came from and when I said Cheshire they would say I thought it was some shire or other. When I am speaking in company now you would think I was some cockney almost. Tell Sambo I am very much pleased with his well written letter and think he was quite right in wanting a whole envelope for it indeed I think it deserved two. Remember me to Bessie Donkeysback and all other interesting old people. I often wonder how everybody is going on. I am sorry Mabury was so foolish to get discharged it would have been a job for life. Give my respects to Mr.Buttermilk I mean Butterworth and Mr.Moss, Jim Hayes and all Hayes and to Mr.Witticker and familly, Mr.Gretton and Mrs. Gretton, Miss Dunnington, Boss Ann and to Cousin James and familly, Bob Williamson and everybody, but most particular of all to Aunt Mary and John Rose. I shall write next mail to those two. I am pretty steady but not one of your eye-rolling sort. You must please excuse my not sending you any presents for we are so anxious to save all the money we can that we dont throw much away, however we will make up for it after a while. I must now finish, letter writing is harder work for me than a days work. I hope you are all well and give my love to Hedley John and Samuel and mother.

This is Monday night I did not know whether I should write any more so thought I would be drawing to a close. I will tell you how we live. Father is the cook and a jolly good cook too, we get pies and puddings every week besides chops and steaks to breakfast and tea to dinner we generally have a pasty each or something like that, as for washing there is very little - 3 shirts, 3 pr socks 3 flannels towels and is all father and I does it in an 1hr. Washing pots and I generally make Phil do but scrub the shanty out myself a fortnight, on the whole we are doing first class and the cheapness is the beauty of it instead of paying 1£ a week each for board and lodging. I should very much like to see you all you must have grown a bonnie handsome girl by this time. I must now say good bye and by next mail I will have a better prepared letter for you.

Your very affectionate brother
Charles Wright

My Dear Aunt Mary,

I hope you are quite well as you look on the photograph, we three are all very well here. I am very much to blame and very ungrateful and very sorry not to have written before, it is all my fault but letter writing is a terror to me. Do not expect to hear anything about our passage out, for my hair turns white every time I think of it. I assure you I was as thin as a shadow of a match when I landed instead of being fat. I am getting stout and fatter now too. I thank you very much for the Tobbaco, it seems I made a mistake thinking it was my people sent it, they never told me different neither. I thought I had drawn on their hard hearts pretty well but after all my trouble of canting and making them laugh I failed to squeeze it out of them. But I shall take no notice in fact I think I punished them pretty well before ever I left.

Auckland is a much finer place than Wellington, the principal St. is Queen and about as broad as Market St. Man. It is a beautiful place too, has 2 parks one a very fine place right in the centre of the city on a hill from the top of it you can see a great way, also the harbour and the sea beyond. We have a good museum with a great many Maori relics in it, a splendid free library full of interesting books and lots of the home papers. There is a large Theatre and a Opera House but they charge so much that if they stand for ever I shall not patronise them.

The Shemale portion of N.Zealanders dress very fashionable and there is a regular war going on in Auckland whether it shall be most fashionable for young ladies to have the hair cut short or not, some you see coming along as if they had a terrible attack of fever or measles. I always give them bald headed customers a wide berth one never knows, others again wear their hair down to their feet almost like a mermaid. Philip belongs to the latter class he takes a pride in growing it down his back and sometimes you cant tell whether he carries ears or collar or not. You can tell Tom Hammond that for a single, strong, young fellow like himself that it is undoubtedly the best thing to come out if he intends to work hard and keep square, but if not just as well stop at home, better, because you can get drunk and for a deal less money, but if a man works hard and is careful he can put money by for instance an ordinary labourer with 8s. a day of 8 hrs can easily put money away 1£ a week and still enjoy himself. Board and Residence is from 17s to 1£ a week, but if two or three fellows get a small 2 roomed house and backhouse it can be done much cheaper. Carpenters get 10s. a day Bricksetters 10s. It is an awkward matter to advise anybody to come out because if things do not turn out well the blame is laid on the shoulders of the advisers, but all I can say is that I dont regret coming in the least, because a working man has a chance here, while in the Old Country if he must live at all respectable he cant save much. Besides there is a sort of a feeling existing here that 1 man is as good as another and a big sight better, all have come out to better themselves and a good many intend it. Give my love to Cousin Mary at Stockport. I hope she will be quite recovered by the time this gets to you, also to Cousin James and Sarah Jane. Remember me to my relations at Manchester and to Mr.Beswick and to Bobby Worth, tell him I expect he is leading the cooks a hard life. I hope he will soon be promoted. Give my love to Aunt Phoebe tell her that dirty lad is 5ft 6" high and as steady as my Grandfathers clock. Give my respects to Miss Vaux and Mr.William Bailey and any decent body you come across. When you see Charles Holt give him kind regards and whatnot tell him I should like to hear how he is going on.

I have had so much bother about them photographs, been taken 3 times, lost 6 or 7 dinners through them that you must not expect me to look very heavenly on the card. I thank you very much for the photo and also for the numberless other presents I have received from time to time and as I said before you are the only person who remembers the poor old devil when he's gone.

I shall see you have your full share of letters anyhow and don't think you are forgotten for I can't forget that the happiest days I ever spent were when I was living with you at Hope Green. Give my love to all at home you all seem so very anxious about my being steady as you call it that it is enough to drive a fellow to drink if he had any money. May the Lord bless all of you not forgetting me.

From your simple but affectionate nephew.
Charles Wright Esq.   Amen

Monday, June 22/85

My Dear Aunt,

I wonder how you are getting on. I got no letters and only one paper last mail. I'll be glad when you can send them to where I live, I don't believe I get one half that are sent. The P.O.Officials are very careless in fact I have seen them give papers away to clear them out.

It is winter now, so far we have had pretty good weather but I fear it is breaking now, today is our shortest day, and your longest. Trade here is rather slack just now, I know several carpenters who have been out of work a month and some longer. I am working myself but the boss is slack. We are working in a suburb called Epsom putting a new storey on a wooden house, we'll finish in about a week and then I think we are to be sent up country to a place called Panamure for a week or two to put up some sheds on a cattle station. Tom Harrison sent word he is coming out, now I wish you to let him know by no means to let any thing I have said be the cause of his coming here because things are not so brisk as they might be especially in the got-a-bit-of-all-sorts-and-no-particular trade line. When a person comes here after reading Emigrant papers and hearing a fellow talk who has managed to get along pretty well, he naturally expects he is going to do the same if not better; if he don't then he is apt to say hard things about the unlucky fellow who has been lucky enough to keep his head above water and say Had it not been for so and so and his infernal lies I'd never been here. Then on the other hand if a fellow warns him before hand he says "O he don't want me to come and soon (you see the troubles of a Pioneer Newchum). However my advice to any intending emigrant (especially those who are going in for big licks and taking the world before them) is if you are doing at all well at home stay there, anyhow in the present case I'd advise him to consult my Father he will then have something reliable to depend on and I'll be clear of his venturesome blood.

I'm very sorry to hear my Mother has this bad thing coming on her. I hope to goodness it aint a cancer or anything of that sort. By her letter I should she is far from being well, she seems weary and depressed in spirits, telling me the churchyards full and all this sort of thing a regular terror aint it. I am glad to hear Philip has got put apprentice to such a good trade although it is not much good here at present, he nearly tires me to death reading his long letters. I tried to get that piece of music for my cousin Sarah Jane but could not, better luck by next mail perhaps, anyhow if it is to be got I'll get it.

I think I'll not say any more now but don't get discontented. I'll send you all plenty of letters and news papers yet besides I'm coming to tell you all about it someday. Give my love to all my people Jack Rose my cousins, yourself and my respects to every body in general more next time from your

Affectionate Nephew
Sir Charles Wright
Good Bye

Alfred, Charles and Philip Wright worked as joiners in Auckland in 1884. They lost work and pay to have this photograph taken in good daylight, to send home to their family, Ann, Martha Ann, Hedley, John and Samuel. Alfred and Philip returned home to their family, at Lowerhouse, Bollington in January 1885.

Charles stayed in Auckland, New Zealand. He married Leah Pattison on 26 May 1886 at St. John's Church, Northcote. This family photo was taken about 1893 with Alfred Hedley, about five years old, posed on the photographer's studio tricycle.

This photograph of Hedley Wright was sent by his foster son, Eric Bandelow in 1983. The family likeness to his cousin, Clifford, is remarkable.
Born on 7 December 1888, Hedley died on 1 November 1982 in his 95th. year.

Dear Mother and Father,

I hope you are all well. Mother, I expect will never be well again, there is one consolation however she will be in heaven, along with Grandfather and Grandmother and little George, it would be a strange heaven where they shut such as she out.

You remember Mr.Ardern he is very ill with the Typhoid fever.
Allens are all right, they have buried their child. I think he is often out of work. Gilbertson I know nothing about. Sam Collier along with his partner Joe Nutt are finishing off a contract alterations to an hotel in Karangahape Road. Robert is about the same in health, I dont think he will ever be better, he often talks of going home, he gets very little work either.

You have no doubt heard of the fearful eruptions at Tarawera and the Hot Lake district above S.E.Aroah and of the great loss of life both of Europeans and Maoris, and property. We believe the worst is over now and that we are comparatively safe although people are leaving Mt.Eden. I myself think that with such a vent as the Lake District has, that Auckland district is safe enough, anyhow I am sending you a special supplement of the Star with a full account of the whole affair and with views of the place before the (bust up) and after.

I am going to tell of something now worse than earthquakes, volcanoes, or almost anything in the history of New Zealand, now, are you ready, keep cool, be prepared for the worst. **I have got married!!!** Yes, its all out now, look in the marriages of the Star I am sending. We were married by our Chaplain at St.Johns Church, Northcote. You will understand that we are not married on the ordinary footing namely renting a house, buying furniture, and all that sort of thing; oh my that would never do, especially on my slender income. I am very comfortably and contentedly fixed. My wife is the only daughter of Joseph and Mary Pattison of Mt. Eden, Mr.Pattison is old and his aim for a long time has been to see his daughter settled in life.   He lives in his own house, owns several allotments round here, and is in easy circumstances generally. We are to be their heirs, for anything we know. We live with them and I am what you may say happy and content.

My wife "Leah is her name" is like the missis of the house, and does most of the work her mother not being very strong, for which they clothe and feed her in fact they could not do without her, whilst I pay 15s a week for board. Our case is an exception to the rule that people dont agree living together for we are all as comfortable and happy as I suppose is possible in this world. For my part I don't see how you can blame me. I am better off than when I was single and certainly a deal more content. I'll send you more particulars next mail or the next but one. Things here are very bad at present but there is every indication of a busy spring. I hope Aunt Mary is well and my cousins at Stockport, and Grandfather and Grandmother and Jack Rose and give my respects to all,

from your affectionate son
Charles Wright

Dear Aunt Mary,

I was surprised at receiving a visit from Dr.Kenderdine the other day. He brought a letter with him, asking me if I knew the writing. I told him I did, then he asked me if I was all right, I told him, yes then he asked me a lot of questions about Macclesfield, he mentioned several families such as Brocklehursts, Martin Swindells and the like. He told me mother was dead, I told him I knew, and was very grieved to hear about it. He said he would write you and let you know I was all right, he showed me your stamp but it was useless. I am living next door to where I was before, only this is Shaddock St, and the other Violet St, this is the way of it

Of course you know by this time that I am married, what do you think about it. The girl I married is Leah Pattison, she is a good girl and an only daughter, living next door I soon scraped an acquaintance which ended in our marriage. We were married at Northcote the other side of the harbour at St.Johns Church, by the Rev.A.J.Hitchcock, Chaplain to the Naval Artillery Brigade of which I am a member. I left the Cavalry it was too expensive. Leah's mother is never well, and on account of this she has to keep house for her, therefore they keep her.

I am very content and happy. I have all my own way about the place, and all agree together. I am sending a portrait of the house from the back. Leah had her portrait taken awhile back but as they were not good ones I am not sending one, we shall both be taken in the summer, then we will send one. That person on the walk is Mrs. Pattison, the person on the verandah steps is Mrs. Nutt, Leahs cousin by marriage. Things are fearfully bad here there are hundreds of unemployed. I am joining the Loyal Orange Lodge, Star of Eden. Mr. Pattison has been Master and wears all the colours of every degree.

I write soon. I will send again soon. I am very proud to see you have been able to retain the Empire whole and have knocked the tree felling rascal out of power whom I believe is a Catholic traitor in disguise. If Home Rule had been granted to Ireland there would have been the greatest civil war ever known. You may believe I was grieved to hear of Mothers death how I regret the pain and sorrow I have caused her in my bad life but all to late now, anyhow she is in heaven and enjoying her reward. Tell Father, Robert, Sam and Allen are all right. I did not give his message to Allen yet, and Hardern is recovering from a serious illness.

Good Bye from
Charles Wright

My Dear Aunt,

You are very kind indeed to write to me and it is as little as I can do to answer it as soon as possible. I hope you are well in health. I suppose you are having pretty cold weather in the Old Country now. It is very hot here. It is Sunday I am lying on the bed with the window open writing to you. It is the window on the right hand of the photograph and even here I am perspiring. The last few weeks I have been working amongst the Maories. The man whom we are building the house for is a full-blooded Maori but so well educated that he speaks the best English I ever heard almost. His father was a Chief and a terrible fighting one in the old days for which he got nearly all his lands comprising of thousands of acres confiscated. His son has taken the English name of William Wilson, his Maori name is Takanina. One of the remants of his fathers estate he lives on and is even now far from being a poor man, he lives like a king surrounded by dozens of Maories who are all his servants, although they never get a penny, plenty to eat and drink and occasional trip to Auckland and they are satisfied. I should think a dozen of them would not do as much work in a day as a European is expected to do in half the time, as one of them observed to me the other day, he says me no like Auckland to much work, thinks I there are a few hundreds in Auckland who don't believe there is enough. Of course we work from light to dark and generally manage to get eleven or twelve hours in the day. In the evening we adjourn into the Maories Wharies or houses for a spell and get the women dancing the haka or war dance or perhaps go for a swim in the little inlet the estate being on the coast. I'll tell you a laughable case I witnessed last Friday. The piccananies or children had been misbehaving themselves some way or other. So Mr. Wilson orders them up for punishment, first he makes one of them bring him a stick about 3 feet long, and places a keg for a seat, then measures off 6 feet from the keg, draws a long line and commands the youngster to come up for punishment. The little imps wear nothing but a shirt and that sometimes minus sleeves or tail, then comes the question Have you been to the Whiteman's house, that is in way of us Carpenters, but he asks the question in Maori. "Ire go wha hu te Pakahia's whare" Ay or kowhi, yes or no. The imp hesitates whack comes the stick on his bare --- he having lifted his remnant shirt to receive 3 blows each, and to see the rolling eyes and sullen visage of them Maori kids would make you laugh after he has gone through the crowd they form a writhing wriggling line until commanded to disperse.

Mrs.Crabtree has not left here yet, she was here yesterday saying she did not know when exactly she will go but in any case not long she says she will open the Budget when she arrives. I hope she will because I can't put much in letters. I thank you gratefully for the kind wishes and advice you send me and so does Leah. You are quite right in saying there are many changes there since I left you. While I think of it there are a troup of real Maories in England at the Exhibition. I think they will travel the country afterwards exhibiting the war dance and such like. I would advise you to see them. I can't write much more as it is church-time, but I must say that I thank you very much indeed for the watch and will be only to glad to accept it and wear it too. I think if you were to pack it in a little box with plenty of wadding and register it too it will come safe enough. Thousands of watches cross the water in this way safely enough and why not this one, whatever the cost is I will refund you. And now my dear Aunt Mary I will wish you good-bye and may God keep and preserve.

I remain
Your loving nephew
Charles Wright

My dear Aunt

You will think it strange this not being written in Charlie's handwriting but he wrote in pencil yesterday and hadn't time to re-write before church and asked me to write it for him, so I wrote this morning and the mail goes out earlier than usual so please excuse this scribbling.

I remain

Your loving niece, Leah B.Wright.

Shaddock St, Eden Terrace
Sun 27/3/1887

My Dear Aunt Mary

I received your letter and also the watch in good order. I was really surprised to find how small and compact it is, my recollections as to its size were quite exaggerated, a more compact and better looking watch I never saw, and I can assure you I prize it more than any present I could own. I have shown it to an expert in watches and he pronounced it to be an English Lever of better workmanship than most made these days. The watch chain and brooch Leah was very gratified to receive, especially as it proved you look upon her with kindness at least. As regards the money I will return it as early as possible. It sounds bad to be making excuses after all your kindness but to tell you the truth I could not send it now, more than half the time since we have been married I have been out of work, but I have started again and may send it next mail. I am very sorry to hear you are in such low circumstances, always being under the impression you were comfortably situated. I only wish I were in a position to help you should not be under the necessity of keeping boarders, perhaps I may some day. I hope you are well in health. I do not believe there is another brooch in the colony like the one you sent. We were having a big time yesterday opening the Free Public Library the largest and best in Australasia but you will read of it in the paper I am sending. Friday week being Good Friday we are to have a monster encampment of volunteers and a sham fight there will be upwards of 5000 of all branches of the service on the ground. I don't think there is any more striking news only the old story of bad trade, of course you know that I am an Orangeman. Good Bye Aunt Mary, we are all pretty well here and hope you are the same. Leah and her Father and Mother send you their best love and I the same,

Charles Wright

Please give my love to my Father and to Martha Ann and the rest of the family and to my cousins at Stockport . Good Bye

---

Eden Terrace
Oct 4/90

My dear Aunt Mary

I thank you very much indeed for the money you so kindly got for me. I can form an idea of the trouble and expense you were put to, and I'm deeply grateful, more so than I can express. We in this country are in a very unsettled state and how it is all going to end I can't make out. Nearly all branches of labour are suspended on account of the seamans strike. We in this city are depending almost entirely on goods brought from the South, therefore their striking and kindred societies such as wharf labourers, carters, wharehousemen etc. causes all trade to be suspended. However it is to be hoped it will soon be settled. The carpenters are getting a little that way now, we have lately formed a union besides the Amalgated Society of Carpenters and Joiners to which I belong, called the Auckland Carpenters Union we are amongst other things going in for a rise of wages. I am at present working at a place called Onehunga 9 miles away for six shillings per day whilst the pick and shovel men are supposed to get eight and wharf men 2 shillings per hour, we who have to find so many tools have to travel all over the country, pay railway fare and have to accept what we can get and be thankful. This great Maritime Strike is nothing to do with this country but owing to the fact of all seamen in these colonies being fedrated, notwithstanding its having originated in N.South Wales, it extends throughout Australasia.

What will be the upshot I dont know there are a many trades affected. We are getting glorious spring wheather just now there is no mistake this is a grand climate but as I heard an Irishman observe the other day what is the good of that if you cant get anything to eat. I suppose at home you are now thinking about ordering the winter coals. Mr.& Mrs.Pattison send their best wishes to you. Mr.Pattison has been laid up in bed for the 14 weeks. I am afraid he wont last long in fact we gave him up several times but he may last the summer now. My wife and little boy are quite well

Your Affectionate Nephew
Charles Wright

_____

From Leah Wright

Shaddock St.
28/10/98

Dear Aunt
We were very much surprised to hear of father's death as we had never heard he was ill. Hedley hasn't wrote to us for some time. I do not know whose fault it is, whether we answered his last letter I really cannot say. Charlie was very cut up, it gave him a shock, what a peculiar thing both parents should die of the same complaint it is a terrible thing. Charlie keeps about the same well and sick off and on, some time ago we had to call in the doctor to him. My mother asked him what was really the matter and he said Asthma and the heart slightly affected he still looks very young only his hair is getting thin, it is a good thing we have no more children. Hedley will be ten this coming 7 Dec. he is a good boy not very big but very much like his father only I think will grow a stronger man. Dear Aunt I suppose we will get full particulars next letter as you didn't give us the date of his death, if it were not for you, we would hear nothing about the Wright family. There is no more to say but we all unite in sending our love.

From your affectionate niece
Leah Wright

_____

Shaddock St.
19 March 1899

Dear Aunt Mary,
We received your welcome letter and the photos from Martha Ann, they are very nice but Martha A. has altered, she has got so thin, they all seem to get thin, Charles is the same they don't seem to take after their mother, and they look so sad in their photos even little Hedley at times has that pensive look. I think they favour their mother in that, in her photo she looks sad, Martha A. little boy looks nice, but I think he must be like his father. I will write a few lines to Martha A. and enclose it in your letter if you will kindly send it to her. I have really no news that would interest her. I sent you and the boys an exhibition number. I hope you recieved it safe. I know you will like it. Charles keeps pretty well, hoping you are the same, little Hedley grows more like his father, he is an obedient boy, and his father is very indulgent, he never corrects him so it is a good thing he is easily managed, he asked me did you send the book, he often talks of you and tells me he will save up to go to England,

he said he has seen a baby somewhere like his little cousin, we were sorry to hear of Hedley, he is a martyr to those fits, there is really no more to say but we all send our best wishes and love to you.

I remain
Your loving niece
Leah Wright

Shaddock St

29 Sept. 1900

Dear Sister,

I received both your letters, but was waiting to receive the bride cake before I answered them; well we got it last Monday and the letter with the sad news of Hedley's death last Wednesday. Charlie was very much upset he said he was always such a quiet lad, and our Hedley reminds him so much of him. I think he is better off than always living in the dread of these everlasting fits. I don't think they are a very strong family. Charlie always seems to be ailing he always puts it down to indigestion. We got a letter from John, he did not mention Samuel either. Aunt Mary will feel Hedley's death very much I am sure. Tell her we were asking for her. I think I wrote last, but tell her to write, Charlie always likes to hear from her. I hope dear sister you will be very happy in your married life and that you won't be handicapped with a lot of children. Our boy is very quiet I think he is like the Wrights quiet and reserved. I am much more lively than Charlie in manner but I have always good health I suppose that is why. Tell Philip he wishes to be remembered to him and always talks of writing. He sometimes gets homesick. I hope Philip will get strong again it is terrible when the men ail. Dear sister excuse this scribble as I always leave my writing to the last minute, remember us to Martha Ann, she never answered our letter, I expect she will some time in the sweet bye and bye.

Now wishing you good by with love to all goodbye from,

Your loving sister
Leah Wright

Leah wrote this letter to her sister-in law Edith (nee Harrop) who married Philip Wright on 21 May 1900. Philip and Edith's granddaughter, Christine Beard (nee Wright), recently found it among her grandfather's papers from the attic.

From Eric Bandelow

9 Manuka St.
Orewa, Hibiscus Coast
Auckland. 14.6.77

Dear Mrs. Wright,

As you will of learnt from your correspondence with Miss Corser, Alfred Hedley, although never married has allways been a Dad to me and may I add a very dear one. In 1926 at the age of 18 months I was the last of quite a few children kindly fostered by his Mother Leah. As they were the only Parents I ever new they became Mum & Dad to me and all my 51 years of time have been all the better for this. Charles Wright for some reason unknown to me, I never met. He and Leah were never together during my time the reason for this I have never enquired as I feel it is not my concern, however, I do think him being away had a great bearing on Mum Wright taking in children to help make ends meet during the hard times although I'm sure she was not helped too much by my parents where ever they were. Another I know nothing about is Philip??? I have never heard him mentioned by either Dad or Mum when she was alive and even now Dad says he never had a brother so this section of the family may remain a mystery.

I trust you don't mind me corresponding with you on Dads behalf. I actually don't mind doing it for him however as pleased as he is to hear from relations and to receive such extensive information of same he is just a little past sitting down and putting pen to paper, and answering in a manner fitting enough for all the news he's received and so with his help I'm doing my best to give you all the information that will be of interest to you.

Charles Wright passed away in 1948 and by the dates on the family tree you sent Dad, he would have been 83 years of age. I do recall Mum and Dad making the funeral arrangements and he was cremated in Auckland.

Leah passed away in 1951 at 81 years of age, this was without a doubt the saddest time of my life. Its very had to explain just how much I loved her. I had been with them almost till the time she died as a matter of fact this added to my sadness as I left the old house to be married and dear old Mum was too ill to attend the wedding. She died just 3 weeks later in the house she had lived in all her life, and this is the very same house Dad is living in now. He was born there and I feel sure he will want to die there as he is hard to move being so independent doing his own cooking washing etc. The 115 year old house is in good repair, although my wife Iris and myself live about 30 miles away. I see him regularly doing the lawns and any of the odd jobs that are a little beyond him, this I really enjoy doing for him for it seems little return for all he and Mum did for me over the years. As you may guess "Jean and Richard" the old house could tell many stories and of the four photos on the Century of Happiness cutting three of the originals are in a beautiful green velvet album in Dads front room (IE) the one of Martha at six years of age, the one when slim waisted at 18 and also the one with the first Baby when she was 30. There are also many other photos in the house and I would guess a lot of them, yourself and family back home in England would also have so you see Hedley has always been in touch with the family he knows so little of, even if only by a few photos to have a look at now and then, and so this recent connection through Miss Corser has been a wonderful and surprising thrill for him I can assure you.

Well Jean & Richard I hope you don't mind me addressing you on a first name basis for after all you are in a manner of speaking a few more foster relations for me for apart from Dad I have no one in N.Z. that I know of, and with my Wife Iris we are the only two people in N.Z. with the uncommon name of Bandelow. It certainly is a contrast in familys mine so small and yours so big!! So why not join hands. I have been a little time answering this for Dad so in order to get it away to you I will close now, hoping in all sincerity I have been able to give you a little of the information that may be of interest to you all at home.

I will have to have a good look around the old house for some more news for you for our next correspondence. So until then I will say cheerio for now from N.Zealand

I remain, Yours faithfully,
Eric Bandelow.

---

9 Manuka St

Orewa,

Hibiscus Coast, N.Z. 1983

Dear Jean & Richard,

May I start the answer to your most welcome and news packed letter, by thanking you for same, and for your Xmas Greetings to us here in New Zealand. I must admit I am the Worlds worst letter writer and although I don't want to make any excuses I do feel a little ashamed at the time that has elapsed since I last wrote to you all.

I feel when reading your letters that the Wright family is a most studious and closely knit unit over there in your home town and because of this it is with sincere sadness that I must inform you of the peacefull passing away of your only tie with New Zealand. Dear old Dad (Alfred Hedley) peacefully went to sleep just prior to his 95th birthday which would have been 7 December. This was from our point of view the end of a long and wonderful life dedicated firstly to his wonderful mother Leah Beatrice while she was alive and then to myself and Iris after her passing in 1951. It is pleasing to add much of the sadness which is always present at funerals was made a lot easier to bear owing to the presence of so many friends he had made through his life many of whom I had never met. The Minister officiating made the remark of how wonderful it was for an old man of 95 to have so many pay their respects.

We had him cremated at his own request and although he never ever joined any Returned Service Associations after his full service in World War One, we had his casket draped with the flag and his ashes were scattered in the Soldier's section of the Cemetery where there is now a bronze plaque bearing his name, Regimental No., etc. forever to his memory. So Iris and myself feel after all he had done for us we are more than happy with our care for him in his latter years and in his final passing however I will never ever be able to explain on paper or in words just how much I loved the only Parents I ever new. Alfred Hedley Wright and his Mother Leah Beatrice. As it was always his wish to return to England, after having been there during W.W.one, Iris and myself are going to try really hard to make the effort ourselves to visit the Old Country in the near future. If and when this eventuates we would love to pay you all a visit and make ourselves known to you.

Well folks after all those lines of sadness I feel I should tell you that Iris and myself are in the best of health spending a lot of time gardening, that is when ever possible, as our Summer has been quite awful. We have had strong gale force winds from the South West for over 3 months and this plays havoc to the shrubs and flowers, etc., however when we see and here the T.V. News from overseas it appears the worlds weather like the world itself is in quite a bad way, so lets all hope and pray for better things to come and we sincerely trust the winter has not treated you too badly where you are.

It would be more than easy to know by your letters that music plays a big part in your lives and although we do not play any instrument at all we are also music lovers and we spend a lot of time dancing to it in the form of Square and Round dancing which although predominately American is very popular the world over and we have met a lot of wonderful people, including Callers from England.

Square dancing itself is done to Country and Western music however the Rounds are very similar to Ball Room and danced to every type of music so there is a great and most enjoyable variety.

I would think you will have noticed what I meant when I said I was the worlds worst letter writer as I feel my writing must be getting a little hard to decipher as the further I go the worse it gets, however I sincerely trust that between you all you will be able to understand it and obtain a little news also.

However I think that's about the lot for just now. We hope all is well with each and everyone of you. May all good things come your way and untill next time God Bless.

Yours faithfully,

Eric & Iris Bandelow

9

Emigration to Canada

Alfred and Philip Wright returned home to Bollington from New Zealand in January 1885. His wife Ann (nee Bennett), developed cancer, from which she died on 18 April 1886. Martha Ann, their 17 year old daughter, cared for her, her father and her younger brothers, in addition to running the home and shop – presumably with the help of a neighbour, Martha Gardiner, of Moss Farm, Lowerhouse. Mary Bennett came to help care for her younger sister Ann and family. Alfred needed to work as joiner/undertaker to support them. Also needing support at Lowerhouse, were Alfred's elderly parents. His father Samuel, aged 74 years and stepmother Ann (nee Greenhalgh) aged 65 years, died within three weeks of each other; Ann on 12 January 1887 and Samuel on 5 February 1887. Three months later, Alfred remarried Martha Gardiner on 4 May 1887 at Prestbury Church.

A Victorian widower was allowed a short three month period of mourning for practical reasons. He needed to remarry, often for convenience, so that his family was cared for, while he worked to finance them all.

Between May1887 and March1889 Alfred had emigrated to Canada with some of his sons. In Martha Ann's letter to Mr and Mrs Brooks, dated 2 March 1889, she writes belatedly to tell them of these three deaths within ten months, and that "my father and some of my brothers have now gone abroad."
They had their photographs taken before they left home. Emigration to Canada was usually by steamship from Liverpool to Halifax, Nova Scotia, from where the Canadian railway transported the immigrants inland.

Alfred and sons farmed in the St. Boniface area, near Dugold, Manitoba. In his letter dated October 1893, Alfred mentions all his sons by name, farming in the fertile Red River Valley. They had taken a copper kettle with them, to boil water on open fires. It returned home coated in soot which was gradually removed by Martha Ann Wright and Mary. Earliest family letters before October 1893 were burnt by Mary Wright who was "tidying up" – to her mother Martha Ann Wright's horror! Martha Ann then hid away the remaining letters from New Zealand, together with her mother's Lady's maid letters, her daguerreotype portrait, tortoiseshell brooch and chatelaine items, in the secret drawer inside the large family oak chest, dated 1790.

Mary Wright told and wrote down some family tradition stories from these early days in Canada. Alfred and son's hand-made wooden shack was blown down in a blizzard. When rebuilt, they left a light burning in the window to help to guide travellers to safe shelter in bad weather. One evening, John and Samuel went for a horse ride. Eventually, they came to a small hillock, from where they could hear the beating of Indian tom toms, and see the smoke from their campfires. They crept nearer and could see the Indian chief and his braves angrily beating their tom toms for war. John and Samuel rode home as quickly as possible.

Sam's father Alfred told him that his grandfather Samuel's older brother, Richard Wright, born 1801, had been a cotton buyer in America. One Sunday afternoon, Richard booked a ticket on the 4.30pm paddle steamer at New Orleans to sail up the Mississippi river to St. Louis. He did not arrive there.

It was presumed that he was robbed, murdered and his body thrown overboard. One of his brothers went to America to try to find him, but found no trace of him or his belongings. Alfred's father Samuel, 1814-1887, wrote a poem "On Embarking for a Foreign Land". Was he writing from personal experience of his older brother Richard or his son Alfred's sailing to New Zealand and Canada?

Alfred had suffered dysentery on the "Lady Jocelyn" and in New Zealand, from his letters to his wife Ann. He became very ill in St. Boniface and was finally admitted to Winnipeg Hospital, where he died of stomach cancer on 5 August 1898. As former joiner-undertaker, Alfred made arrangements for his own funeral. His coffin was made of white oak and carried on their own wagon drawn by two horses which were driven by two friends. Mr Jack, the minister, took the funeral and Alfred was buried in Moose nose graveyard.

Hedley was born on 18 October 1872 in the Flash Lane cottage. He suffered from epilepsy. He attended Lowerhouse Day School and his school certificate records that he passed the IV standard at the examination of this school in November 1882 when he was 10 years old. Aged 16 years, he emigrated to Canada in 1888 with his father and brothers. Hedley was photographed with their dog, Rover, before he left home. By the time of Samuel's letter, written on 7 January 1899, Hedley's epilepsy had deteriorated and he died in Winnipeg in 1900.

Philip was born on 8 February 1871 in the cottage in Flash Lane. In the 1871 census, living with their family was Aunt Mary Bennett, who came to help her sister, Ann and Alfred after the birth. There were two other young children, Charles aged 6 years who appears to have been hyperactive, following his lumbar abscess when 4½ years old, and 2 year old Martha Ann. Philip had an adventurous youth, sailing the world with his father and brother Charles - to New Zealand and back when he was 12 to 15 years old. Then, aged 17 years he emigrated to Canada for 10 years, until he was 27 years old. Philip did not take to farming and after seeding in 1893, he left the family farm to work for the Ogilvie Milling Company in Winnipeg. However, he had returned to his family before 13 December 1896, when he wrote to his sister Martha Ann. He described the cold weather and blizzards of November and their earlier good wheat crop. He wished to be remembered to family members and the Harrop family hoping that "Edith had not died of a broken heart". Philip returned home to Bollington in 1897 by working his passage on a cattle boat. He worked in the corn business of his brother-in-law, Richard Wright of 13-15 Shrigley Road. His sister, Martha Ann gave birth to their first child, Isaac Clifford on 8 December 1897. Philip joined Stockport Borough Police on 24 October 1898 and lived at 68 Freemantle Street, Stockport. Philip renewed his courtship of Edith Harrop and they married on 21 May 1900. They had one son, Norman Hedley, born 28 January 1912, who later became editor of the Stockport Express. From Philip's police record, we learn that he was promoted to "one stripe rank" 1908-1914. On 3 December 1909, he received 2s 6d reward for "apprehending a felon". He was promoted to Acting Sergeant in 1919 and to Sergeant in 1920 until his retirement in 1926, after 28 years exemplary service. He was an active member of the RSPCC for 27 years. After his wife Edith died in 1940, Philip went to live with his son Norman, his wife Elsie and granddaughter Christine. Philip died aged 87 years on 11 May 1958.

After their father Alfred and Hedley's deaths in Winnipeg and Philip's return to England, John and Samuel travelled west to Lanigan, Saskatchewan. They first found work in a grocery store. In 1904 they took up homesteads to farm. John was born on 3 December 1874 in the cottage on Flash Lane. John's favourite interest was music. He was a self-taught violinist, who played in the Lanigan orchestra in 1913. Previously in Winnipeg, he had been a member of the band of the Winnipeg 90th Regiment. He also composed music and played the flute. He was an avid reader. John farmed all his life and was a member of the United Growers' Association. He took a keen interest in community affairs and was a school governor of Stoner Rest School. He was a member of the Lanigan Masons' Lodge No 84. John married Freida Walta on 17 June 1921 at Yorkton. Freida was born on 7 May 1891 in Lodz, Poland. Her parents, of German parentage, had a general store in Fabienz, Poland. The family came to Canada in June 1908 and lived in Yorkton, Saskatchewan for a time. They moved to Philadelphia, Pennsylvania U.S.A.

Whilst visiting her sister and family in Lanigan, Freida met John and they married on 17 June 1921. Freida's interests were gardening and needlework. John and Freida had three daughters, Elsie b1922, Helene b1924 and Dorothy b1929. They all married but had no children. John and Samuel's sister, Martha Ann Wright, aged 90 years, with her daughter Mary and son-in-law Albert Weate, visited relatives in Canada in June 1958. The family group photograph was taken outside John and Freida's home in Lanigan. John Wright died on 18 September 1960. The funeral service was held at Lanigan United Church and he was buried in Lanigan cemetery.

Samuel Wright was born on 21 May 1876 in Water Street, Bollington. After emigrating to Canada, and moving to Lanigan from Winnipeg with his brother John, they first found work in a grocery store. Sam filed for a homestead North-east of Lanigan in 1905. He married Ada Kitchen of Wolverhampton in 1910. Sam and Ada moved to Bandalor, Saskatchewan where he took over the butcher's shop. Later they took over the Jansen Hotel, where they stayed for 25 years. They then bought the Borden Hotel, Saskatchewan. They sold out and bought an Autocourt in Mission City, B.C. where they retired. Here they celebrated their Golden Wedding Anniversary in 1960. On retirement, they returned to England to Ada's family in Wolverhampton for 2 years. Sam was taken ill there, and they decided to return to Lanigan, Canada in August 1965. Sam died in Lanigan Hospital on 27 September 1965. He was buried in a grave next to his brother John's in Lanigan cemetery. Ada was born in Wolverhampton on 21 October 1888. She took a keen interest in church affairs and loved company. She was 87 years old when she died in 1975.

Elsie and Helene, then Helene and her husband Erwin Hein, visited relatives in Bollington in 1970s and early 1980s. Helene provided these family details about their parents and Uncle Sam and Aunt Ada. We exchange Christmas cards and letters annually. In 2004, Helene and Dorothy have deposited three family photographs with their Heritage Centre: one of their parents John and Freida, one of Uncle Sam and Aunt Ada and the third one of the Lanigan orchestra in 1913 where John was a violinist.

Philip Wright in Stockport Borough Police uniform. He was promoted to Sergeant in 1920.

In his youth he sailed to New Zealand and Canada with his father and brothers. He returned to England, aged 26 years, in 1897 and joined Stockport Borough Police Force in October 1898. He married Edith Harrop in 1900 and had one son, Norman.

John Wright settled in Canada with his brother Samuel who married Ada (nee Kitchen). John and his wife Freida (nee Walta), had three daughters, Elsie, Helene and Dorothy.

Martha Ann Wright, aged 90 years, with her daughter, Mary, and son-in-law, Albert Weate, visited her brothers, John and Samuel, in Canada in June 1958. This family group photograph was taken outside John and Freida's home in Lanigan, Saskatchewan.

Back row:-	Mary (56), Albert (61), Samuel (81)
Centre row:-	John (84), Freida (67)
Front row:-	Martha Ann (90), Ada (70), Helene (34)

10

Letters From Canada

Suthwyn P.O.
Man, Canada
Oct 1893

Richard Wright Esq.

Dear Cousin and Son in Law,

Your letter of the 8 inst to hand last Tuesday. I was pleased with the kindly remembrance you have of us and of the good feeling and wishes conveyed to us by it and thank you.

With respect to the event you notify us of I sincerely hope that you may be as well satisfied with your choice as I was with Martha Ann's mother. I do not think M A could have done better and had her poor mother been alive I feel sure that it would have had her approval as it has mine and I am sure too it would have pleased my father.

I am glad that business continues good with you and hope that you may be blessed with a long and prosperous and happy married life.

I have thought ere this that the comforts and enjoyments of life which your family has experienced so long is largely and very largely too due to the integrity and devotion to God on the part of your father. "They that honour me I will honour" and I believe firmly that in your case God has not gone back on his word.

In making this remark I do not wish to disparage your ability and foresight as a shopkeeper, but you will remember the words of the hymn "Unless the Lord conduct the plan, the best concerted schemes are vain and never can succeed".

Your father told me but some two or three days before his death that if he had his life to live over again it should be given more to the spiritual welfare of his family and less to the gathering together of money. As he lay on his death bed he could fully see the depth and vastness of the meaning of the words "what shall it profit a man if he shall gain the world and lose his soul" with which words he finished up his advice to me. I was fond of your father and I reverence his memory.

As regards ourselves I am thankful to say that we are all in good health; poor Hedley is still a subject of epilepsy I am sorry to say; he has a fit I suppose on an average once a week; and I have pretty nearly come to the conclusion that he has them for life; in other respects he is a strong and hearty young fellow, he was 21 yrs old last Sunday.

I am thankful too to tell you that we have had a good crop. Hay has been exceedingly abundant. I think there has been this year as much grass as the previous years we have been here put together. We have close upon 5,000 bushels of grain. and our oat crop would have been much heavier if I had had the money to have bought new seed for all the land we had under oats. The oat crop was light last year generally and I was obliged much against my will to sow our own seed, which have given a crop of 50 bushels to the acre weighing only 34 lbs to the measured bushel; whilst the American Banner oats we bought have yielded 80 bushels to the acre weighing 45 lbs to the measured bushel. All grain is sold by weight 34 lbs of oats to the bus. 60 for wheat, and 48 barley.

So you see it is a matter of the first importance that the very best seed only should be used, as the labour of cultivation is the same for a poor yield as a good one. Since spring there has been some kind of fatal disease in the Province amongst horses and we can scarcely speak to a farmer that has not lost one or more. We have lost a fine young horse of great promise from this ailment which nobody seems to understand. The vets can do no good to them. They seem gradually to waste away finishing up with diarrhoea which nothing can stop. Stock are exceptionally healthy in this country, especially cattle. We have lost two horses since we began farming and have had a good colt killed by lightening; but we have only lost one cow and she died in calving.

Both the boys and I like the free and independent life of a farmer, when I was in Bollington I was continually oppressed with the feeling that I had not room enough, a "kinder sort" of feeling of confinement. Here on the broad prairie we can take in thousands of acres in a glance in any direction, a sea of land as it were. But Philip though he likes the country has never taken kindly to farming, and he has abandoned it for a permanent situation in the city, he is working for the Ogilvie Milling Co; he left us after we had got through seeding.

Winnipeg continues to grow each year, large and costly buildings and erections of a humbler stamp go up. The streets have as fine an electric car service as can be found anywhere. I hear that much American money is invested in the city, and Americans are a go-ahead people. And as the city grows land around it must of necessity increase in value as time goes on; and situated as we are as some describe it in the famous Red River Valley our land cannot always remain at its present value.

This would be a grand country if summer frosts did not trouble the grain; this year we had no frost nor last year but two years ago 1400 dollars scarcely covered the damage done to our grain by frost. The trouble at present is the low price at which grain sells at, and there does not seem a much better prospect of better prices in the near future. The best wheat is only worth in Winnipeg 49 cts per bus of 60 lbs.

I should like Martha Ann to get all my papers from Lower House, such as birth registers and any writing she may find of her own mothers. I lost her mothers letters to me when in New Zealand, in the fire when our house was burnt here. The papers I want were in the small drawers of the dressing and wash tables in the large bedroom. There is some old papers of my fathers wrapped in brown paper in the wash stand drawer, and any writings of mine or her mothers or my fathers that she can find I wish her to bring away, and her mothers black silk mantle for which I have a special regard I want away.
I hope to make a trip over in a few years to fetch my clock and picture and some other things that it was never my intention to lose possession of. I want you to have in your keeping the family bible Aunt Mary gave her mother and me, and the large picture of her mother I want away. If you will be good enough to oblige me in this matter I will thank you.

I am glad that a difficulty has arisen in sending the fiddle off, as it would cost more in carriage and duty than it is worth. I grumbled at the boys sending for it. John can play his flute well but I am not particularly anxious that they fiddle their time away, as there is something always waiting to be done.
We bought a washing machine and a wringer yesterday as we have a big wash on hand. Samuel describes it as a tremendous big wash.
With my kindest regards to my Aunt and Cousins.

I remain
Yours very sincerely
Alfred Wright

P.S. Please tell M A to bring away the metal tea pots and the old 'forget me not' china that are in the cupboard and the wooden butter bowl, and the horses head over the dresser. The piano belongs to M A.

The event referred to in paragraph 2 is the wedding of Richard and Martha Ann on 18 October 1893.

Suthwyn P.O.
Man.
Decr.31 1894

My dear Sister in Law   (Mary Bennett)

I thought probably you would prefer knowing the latest news concerning Hedley. As you have been informed from time to time of the continuance of his fits I desire to say that the result of them which I have been long expecting has at last come, and that is insanity. For the past 4 years or so his memory has been poor and continually getting worse, and I have noticed too the gradual weakening of his mind. His fits especially of late have been often; oftener than I like to tell you, and very severe; and last thursday night his mind failed altogether, except for about an hour yesterday Sunday when he seemed rational. The doctor says there is no hope for him, and wants us to take him to the asylum and he is so very strong and unmanageable. But my heart revolts against the thought of parting with him to be under the control of others. I have looked after him as best I could all along and shall if possible to the end, which I do not think by present appearances is very far off.

The one theme of his talk is of going to heaven and wants you and all of us to be with his mother there. He is often asking me to write you about this.

This Mary is sorrowful news to write. With my best wishes for you.

From your affectionate brother in law
Alfred Wright
The boys send their love to you.

Suthwyn P.O.
Manitoba
Dec 13/96

Dear Sister   (Martha Ann)

It is with much pleasure I write these few lines to you as I often think of you and the times we had together in the old home. I being no hand at writing you must excuse the long intervals between letters but Christmas is coming soon so I will attempt to pen a few lines to reach you about holiday time. Of course Christmas does not make much difference here (from a worldly view) except we may kill a turkey and eat it to celebrate the event, the day comes and goes like any other as far as a holiday is concerned, we may chance have a few visitors but it is not likely, so I dont look forward to it like I once did. The weather of late has been extremely cold and the month of november will be a month long to be remembered by settlers of North West America. The cold unsettled weather wound up with a genuine blizzard which commenced on the 24 lasted 3 days such a one we dont care to see again, and I see by the papers that lots of unfortunate farmers who happened to be away from home perished in seeking places of shelter from the storm, and there is even in Winnipeg Hospital lots of cases of frost-bites losing fingers and toes and even legs by the excessive cold of late. One case which strikes me just now is of a farmer going from the house to the barn during the storm got baffled by it his body was found on a snowbank about 2 miles south of his house. I can easily understand that as by what S and I experienced last winter, having decided to go for a load of hay we reached the stack alright but on looking around we saw a storm coming up so we left the stack without a load and we had not gone far when a gust of wind caught the hay rack which was 8 foot wide and 14 feet long, and dumped us off rack and all, the already scared team made off which way we could not tell as the storm was on us, and it took us all our time to watch ourselves but instinct seemed to tell us which way to go so we got home alright. John had already found the horses which were stranded with the sleigh on the top of a 4ft 6" fence post which was showing through the snow close to home and had began to get anxious about us. You must know the result of these storms never get in the papers fully as it would hurt immigration and again the result is not known till the snow melts in spring even then supposing the wolves don't get the bodies.

We lost a fine Clyde mare by being gored to death the other day she was in harness at the time it happened. The bull who is an Ayrshire was turned out for exercise, but he meant mischief so going up to her he plunged his right horn into her stomach killing her almost instantly. I stood on opposite side of her never dreaming he was going to do for her, as all bulls are generally quiet in winter. I heard the thud which was almost like the sound of a drum of course I could not see what was going on directly on the other side of her so am not to blame in any way. The bull is a thorough-bred we got him in exchange for ours which is also pure bred Ayrshire and we had intended to de-horn him in the spring as we had also done our own, but to get even with him we sawed them off the day of the mischief.

We had a fair crop of wheat this season the prices are now averaging 70 cents so we can't complain but oats was not worth the thrashing so we are feeding them in the sheaf we had no prairie fire so we get some benefit from the farm this year.

We are all well here alive and kicking as you say at home even in spite of the cold. Remember me to all the folks around home even to the Harrops tell me what has become of dear Edith whether she had died of a broken heart or not. I also see by a paper some of you sent me that Miss L.Hibbert of Tytherington got 1st prize for butter making at the Adlington show which must be quite a honor. How is Aunt Grace and mother keeping this winter give them my best respects also to the other lady I forget her name not forgetting Aunt Mary. I sent you some papers awhile which I hope got alright. Hedley also sent your husband one so I will be very much pleased to receive from you any papers or periodicals you may think proper to send, as it is very monotonous out here in the winter and again our news is all old to you when we get it. So I must conclude as it is bed-time hoping you are keeping well and prospering.

Wishing you and yours a merry Christmas and Happy New Year

Philip Wright

Suthwyn P.O.
Manitoba
Jan 7 1897

Dear Aunt Mary,

On Christmas day I received your last letter dated Dec 9 the same day I received one from Charles wife dated Nov 27 something unusual to get a letter from them. They are very backward in writing to you. In their letter they say how brisk things are there, and that they are better off now than ever they were, she says what a brave little boy young Hedley is and how he can hold "his own" with the bigger boys at school. I say he will have to be careful or some of the days he will be running home with a black eye or with a broken nose or something. I answered their letter a few days ago. Since beginning this letter I have received two Macclesfield Couriers, there is some very interesting news in them. I see in one of them that eggs are six and seven for a shilling, but eggs are very scarce here, our hens are only laying one or two every now and again we killed most of them off for Christmas. Butter is selling here for twenty two and twenty five cents a pound, we are not making very much now. I have not been very well just lately, my father tells me that last week I dropped down four times. I did not know at all about them and I did not hurt myself at all. I think the fits generally come on in the night time or very early morning. Oh if I was only free of them what a blessing it would be. Many a time have I prayed to God that He would cleanse me of my afflictions, and still they keep clinging to me, but what God sends is best. I do not use tobacco in any shape or form and I do not use spirit or beer at all and hope I never shall do. The weather here is very changeable, about New Year we had rain and lots of it then a sharp frost and everything was iced over since then there has been two blizzards blinding snow storms. The weather is very cold; before Christmas we had a long spell of warm weather but at Christmas it changed for the worst. Our cattle and horses are all well but this last summer we have lost two horses, one was killed by the bull, he gored him, since then we have taken his horns off and a few of the milking cattle. Father believes in having all the stock dehorned. Samuel is down in the bush, he is taking out 200 rails for fencing. I think he would rather be out on the roads with the horses than at home looking after the cattle. I am at home all the time very seldom that I go away except Sundays and then it is to the School house to hear the minister's sermon. This winter father has been at work making a buggy to take the butter into town with enclosed. He has given it its first coat of paint, and intends giving it four coats. Philip has been trying to trap some wolves but at present he has not been successful, he has shot three or four rabbits. On New Years day I received a card from Macclesfield dated Dec 16. I cannot form any idea from who it came. Did you send it me and there was a very nice verse on it and ten cents to pay on the envelope for postage.
In conclusion I must say that I wish you a very Happy and Prosperous New Year and that your health will be good. We are all in good health here (excepting my fits) and I am sure all join in sending you most "kindly greetings"

from your most
affectionate nephew
Hedley Wright

Dear Martha Ann,

I thought that I would try and write a few lines to you just to let you know that I am still living. I don't know what kind of a Christmas you have been spending but it has been very quiet one for us. Hedley received a very nice letter from you a short time ago but has been unable to answer it as yet. I am very sorry to say he has been very sick of late, he had nine very bad fits one day which upset him entirely he was unconscious for about four days after, then when he came he complained of terrible pains in his sides and legs he could not bear any one to touch him at all, but he is able to be around again now. I expect he will be writing soon so he will tell you all about it.

Well Martha Ann I am sure you would be surprised to hear of Fathers death it came like a shock to all of us he was only ill about three weeks till he was in his grave. I only saw him about three times after he left home so you see we did not have much time for conversation with him they only allow you to stay one hour and that seems to go like five minutes. I think he expected death after he had been in there about two weeks for he gave me the measurement of his coffin for he wished to have a good solid oak one and a few days later we called and we were quite struck when we went in he just looked like a dead corpse we went up to his bed side and said a few words to him and he knew us quite well then we read a few chapters out of John and prayed with him and he asked god to relieve him of his suffering. Then he thanked us and said he had not been able to read for about a week, we asked him if he was prepared to meet God he said yes I have made my peace with God. I asked him if there was any message to send home he said you can write and tell them I am very ill. We asked him if there was any business he would like to have done he said no I leave everything to you boys do the best you can I am done with it now so John stayed in over night with him and he died next morning at about half past ten.

I see by your last letter that Aunt Grace is very sick but I suppose it is only what we might expect when one gets to such a ripe old age. I am sure it is very kind of Mother to be looking after her so for I know she will have her hands full with the shop. She will hardly know how to turn. I see also that Mr.Philip has joined the Stockport police force I thought that would have been one of the last jobs he would have gone to I think he as tried most everything going it is high time he settled down to something if he is ever going to make anything out in life. I see that he his still keeping company with Miss Harrop does he ever say what his intentions are. Well there seems to be very little news around here threshing is just about completed the farmers are losing very heavy on their crops on account of the heavy rains this fall all they are pay for wheat is from 1 shilling to two English for wheat which is leaving a very small margin for profit things are very dull at present here, fresh butter is only worth from 15 cts so for a 1 dairy butter hay is the only thing that is selling well at present it is worth from 5$ to 7$ a ton they expect it will be worth about 10$ in the spring. Philip asked for a sample of our grain but it is not worth sending on account of it being bleached with the heavy rains. I would be very glad if Richard would send me a sample of oats and horse beans in a paper I expect to be going to the Bush in a week or two with the team as I want to take out some building timber I expect to be about a month at it. I took a lot out last winter. You can tell Philip the south eastern railway is running now and the Rat Portage Timber company has bought that big plow field on the point near the bridge they are going to build a large mill there they expect to cut about 50 million ft of lumber in the season and employ 400 men. Well I must bring this scribble to a close as it is getting Late. Please send us a photo of your little boy I forget his name as I would like to see him.

From your loving Brother
Samuel Wright

My dear Mother and Sister

I must apologise for not having written before this. The news that I have to say is trouble. Three weeks ago yesterday father went into the Hospital to see if the doctors could find what was the matter with him as his stomach had been troubling him all summer the doctors made an examination of him, and found that the trouble was a tumour in the wall of the stomach, and that he would have to go through an operation before he could find any relief, but since he has been in the Hospital he has got so weak that they would not venture with the operation. The doctors sent us word this evening that if we wanted to see him we had better go as he was sinking very rapidly. John has gone tonight and I and Samuel was going tomorrow. Would you kindly let Aunt Mary and Philip know. I must now conclude as it is very late.

I still remain your loving son and brother.
Hedley.

———————————————————

Suthwyn Aug. 5 1898

Dear Mother and sister

Father died this morning. I and John and Samuel was there last on Thursday. John stayed on Thursday night and was with him when he died (friday morning about ten o'clock) he was quite bright in his mind and speaking to the last. He died in a sleep. The funeral was on the following sunday to the Moose Nose Cemetery. Mr Jacks conducted the service at our house, there was a great many people at the funeral, it passed off peaceably.

Mr.McIntyre acted as the Undertaker. The pall bearers were Mr.Stewart, Mr.McIntyre, Mr.Collins, Mr.Baxter, Mr.Sutherland and Mr.Barkwell. Mrs.Baxter did a great deal of work for us, in the form of scrubbing and cleaning round. Mr.McIntyre worked very

The end of Hedley's postscript letter is missing

My dear Aunt Mary

Hedley wrote a letter a week ago to Shrigley road relating the sad event which has recently befallen us. His letter may not reach you before this but however in either case no doubt it will be a surprise to you. Father died on the 5th of this month, he had only been in the Winnipeg General hospital little more than 3 weeks when he passed away. I believe Hedley said the cause was a tumor in his letter, but worse than that, it was the dreadful cancer. The doctors thought when he went in there that it was a tumor if nothing worse, but in conversation with the head doctor (Doctor Moody) after he said that it was cancer on the stomach. Probably if he had gone to the hospital about 3 months ago they might have done something for him as they are very clever there.

When father went in there they thought they could build him up some so as to better stand the operation, but instead he gradually got worse. On the Monday before he died the doctors held a consultation to decide whether to operate or not three was for and 3 against and Moody on whom all responsibility would fall decided against so there was no operation.

Possibly when he went in it might have been successful but when he got so weak. I feel certain myself that he would never have got through the operation and I would much rather he died as he did than to have died under the operation. They injected morphine into his arm which prevented no doubt a great deal of suffering. The doctors and nurses were very kind to him except one a Nurse Stewart who at first neglected him. When I used to go in he complained of sleeplessness and nothing that he would take would stay down. Brandy that used to give him relief when at home would not agree with him there then he took a fancy for beer, they had some bottled Bass's beer which he said was good, but not much of that stayed down and he got to dislike it and towards the last all he wanted was water every few minutes which came back soon after taken. Father died at about 10 minutes to ten in the morning, his mind remaining clear to the last. As I went in about half past eight he spoke to me and said he was comfortable.

Before father died he made a plan for his coffin and gave all measurements on a slip of paper and wished Brown and Rutherford to make his coffin and to be made of white oak. Mr. Jay and Mr. Hall had to do with the making of it and did it well plain but well made. The wood was nicely oiled with a narrow black mould round the lid, six nice handles white and white metal plate on which was the inscription with name and when born and when died.

The funeral was on the Sunday and Mr. Jack the resident minister attended. There was a good attendance of neighbours no less than 17 vehicles leaving the house and 15 arrived at the Moose-nose graveyard. In accordance with his wish he was taken in a waggon drawn by Frank and Minnie. John Thompson and Baxters brother-in-law driving. Mr. McIntyre, Stewart, Sutherland, Collins, Barkwell and Baxter were the pallbears. We started at about half-past two and got back in good time to do the evenings work. I might here state that Father died trusting in Jesus and that he was anxious to go. Mr. McIntyre was very kind also was Mr. and Mrs. Baxter.

I have not been very well myself just lately complaining of a pain in my side. Dr. Moody said he would examine me any time I went in. I feel better now so don't think I will go.

We have had a very wet haying time, most people have not got nearly enough to do there and the harvest is nearly on. We are getting the binder ready to work this morning to cut some barley on Barrowclough's and this week we shall commence cutting wheat and be able to go right on crops are good all round and if frost keeps away the quality will be good. Philip will explain to you anything you may not know. With love to you all. I'll conclude trusting you are in good health.

I remain your loving nephew.
John.

Jansen P.O.
Sask.
March 29 1938

Dear M.A.

Many thanks for your welcome letter so I thought I would drop you a line too. There is not much news things have been very bad out here the whole country side is out on relief the crops was a total failure no feed for stock or grain and the Dominion Govt. is financing the farmers seed for this year. The heat and hot winds just cooked everything up last year so it is to be hoped that this year will be better if this crop fails then the country is done there is no money stirring at all the Govt. of this Province is about Bankrupt only they do not admit I think there will be an Election in June they will have to go to the country again.

Am enclosing a few snap shots of John's children and Ada and myself. John's eldest girl has been with us since Xmas. John was here last week for a day or two and looking after seed grain from the Municipality.

Was very sorry M.A. to hear of Philip's sickness I would have wrote but do not know his correct address.

You refer in your letter about J.Ratcliffes Quarries, I don't know which of them he bought. May be property over there is like it is here, a liability on your hands farms here you cannot give away there is none changing hands big firms have gone out of Business. Lots of wholesalers have gone smash no money, they tell me about 75pc of the retail stores are broke, to many Book accts, cattle and stock realises nothing to day fresh eggs - 15 cts or 7d a doz. butter is a shilling a pound it is scarce on acct of the Govt last fall making the farmers sell there cattle on acct of feed. The Govt last fall took thousands of cattle at 1ct a pound and they went straight for slaughter there must be a lot of canned meat some where. I think a lot of it must have gone to Japan or China for the armies.

You said you was sending a paper but it as not arrived at present. I hope it does for I like to read the news, and what is going on over there. I am trying to get Elsie to enclose a few lines to you she is a fine young girl now I think she is 16 yrs old.

Well I think I will have to draw to close Hoping you are all well.
Love to Nellie, and the Boys and there families, also yourself

from your loving
Brother
Sam Wright

Lanigan, Sask.
November 25 - 1942.

My dear Martha Ann,

I am writing this letter in the hope it will reach you before Christmas. Ordinarily, there would be plenty of time, but as things are, one does not know. Nevertheless it is wonderful how so much mail and other goods have reached their destination.

How are you keeping? I do hope you have had no recurrence of the attack you wrote about, and are taking good care of yourself. As for ourselves we have been keeping pretty well, beyond the ordinary minor complaints one seems subject to.

We have finished a very good year as far as the crops are concerned and with, on the whole, fair prices. But the difficulty is to sell. The government has imposed quotas on the sale of all grains with the exception of flax. And so far it has been 8 bushels for wheat, and 10 bushels to the acre for oats and barley respectively, with the consequent slowing up of business in the West. The crops were late in ripening this year, and as a result the harvesting and threshing was late. In fact there is much grain still unthreshed throughout the country and will probably remain out in the stook until spring. There is much tough grain and the grades none too good. Because of the increased rainfall this past summer the pastures were good and water more plentiful in the wells. Just as a little comparison with the prices for farm products at home, I will quote a few, locally. No. 3 wheat $67\frac{3}{4}$ cents, Feed oats 30 cents. Barley 1 feed 43 cents per bushel. Potatoes $1.00 per hundred weight. No.1 Turkey 22 cents lb. dressed. No.1 fowl 16 cents, eggs average about 35 cents per dozen. Dressed pigs No. 1 bacon $15.35 per hundred at Winnipeg. Horses are scarcely saleable, but cattle command a good price in the various grades. Cream (special) is 39 cents per lb. butter fat including the 6 cents bonus given by the Federal government. These prices are the best experienced for years.

Sam'l came down from Jansen with team and wagon to help me with the threshing, and I was glad of it as farm help is so scarce.

I was to have a dug-out made this summer 150 x 60 x 12 feet deep but when the men were ready to come the ground was too wet, and since then they have had so much work they could not get here before freeze-up. The work is done with a heavy caterpiller engine. The purpose of the dug-out is to create a reservoir of snow and rain water for stock, and comes under the Prarie Farm Rehabilitation Act, and is done at a cheap rate for the farmers who need them.

Elsie is now in Vancouver B.C to try her luck there. I should have liked her to join the Women's Auxiliary of the Air Force. She was rather hesitant, so I did not press her. Helene is at Jansen helping her Aunty Ada. She is much better now than she was when I wrote you last. Dorothy is still going to school but has had to stay at home on account of the cold stormy weather. I regret that I could not afford them further advanced education. Even as it is, they were handicapped by being so far from school.
The news from the battle front is encouraging. I had the pleasure of listening to Mr. Wendel Wilkie this evening when he spoke at a meeting in Toronto in aid of the "Help to Russia" fund. A splendid address given by a very popular man. We enjoy listening to the News-Reel broadcast from London each night at 9 o'clock. It's wonderful how, when reception is good, we get news direct from Russia and Africa through them. A few nights ago I called Dorothy to listen to the tanks and other vehicles roaring past - going into action as the correspondent was speaking.

Well Martha Ann I must close this rambling letter, and with the hope that you and all of you are in the best of health, and wishing you and yours a Happy Christmas and a Prosperous New Year. I am, your

Affectionate brother, John.

Jansen, Saskatchewan
June 2/47

Dear Auntie Martha and Mary,

I received the lovely cushion tops a few days ago. They are very pretty and green is one of my favorite colours. Thank you very much.

I have been married over six months. How quickly time flies for it really doesn't seem that long. We live on a farm one mile from Jansen. I have all the garden in and is coming along quite nice. We have two hundred and thirty young chickens which are five weeks old. So with one thing or another it keeps me busy.

Erwin and I went home yesterday to see Mother and Daddy. It was nice to be home again for a few hours. Daddy was down at Borden for Uncle Sam's birthday. Auntie Ada hasn't been very well. A short time ago she had a clot of blood on the brain and was unconscious for some time, but she is feeling better again.

To Martha Ann Wright & Evelyn Mary Wright, m. Albert Weate from Helene Wright (John's daughter) m. Erwin Hein 22 Nov 1946
The end of this letter is missing.

Box 119, Lanigan, Sask, Canada.
November 24 - 1957

Dear Martha Ann,

We were so glad to receive your letter a few days ago and to know that you are well and, apparently, busy as usual. What a wonderful thing to have accomplished what you have done in completing the task you set for yourself referring, of course, to your personal efforts to raise £100.00 as a gift to the Chapel. It is something to be proud of and we congratulate you on your success. Your letter took just 18 days to reach here. We were sorry to learn that Philip is not doing so well, but glad to know that he is living at a nice place and in good hands.

The holiday to Scotland did you good, no doubt. The change of air and scenery, combined with the friendliness of the people would all add to that effect. You know there are many Scots in Canada. The mother of our present queen stated when she and King George visited Canada, that she had never seen so many Scots before. May be she was exaggerating a little. You know, I have come across people by the name of Wright, both Irish and Scotch who thought I must be one or the other because my name was Wright. Of course they were mistaken. The name is as English as can be and are proud of it.

The weather this past summer was rather dry here, consequently there were short crops in some parts of the province, but the quality of the grain is good. The marketing problem is not as yet solved. Since the new government (conservative) came to power it would seem they are making a greater effort to overcome them. The government is making an advance payment to farmers of 50 cents a bushel of wheat, up to 6 bushels per acre for this year's wheat stored on the farms, and to lesser amounts for oats and barley. This will come into effect tomorrow. It is also free from interest. This will be of help temporarily, but is admitted as no solution. Because of the dry weather our garden was not as good as usual. The soil in Lanigan is much lighter than the soil of the farm. Helene's husband Erwin is leasing our farm.

Received a letter from Elsie yesterday with quite an account of preparations for her wedding scheduled for December 7. Her name will be Webb, and they will be married in the Chapel of the United Church. Mr. Charles Webb is the proprietor of a shoe store with repairing of shoes in connection. They visited us in the summer. At a shower the other evening given by a friend of Elsie, one item was a collection of canned goods, and what do you think - they had taken the labels off them. They seemed to think it was a good joke.

Dorothy is working at the University of Saskcatchewan telephone switchboard now. She got the position by the recommendation of a Mr. Black, the regional manager of the Government telephone system. She had given up the telephone business and was at home for a time when he 'phoned to her to ask her if she would be interested, if so, he would speak for her. She accepted and is in charge with 3 or 4 girls under her. What pleases D is that there is no night work and a 5 day week. While waiting for the operating she was helping to check the arrival of students to the University. At present there are over 9,000. Well Martha Ann "Wishing you and yours 'A very Happy Christmas and a prosperous New Year' and to Philip and family too if there is a chance of letting them know. Pleased to say we are well.

Affectionately,
John & Freda
Parents of Elsie, Helene and Dorothy Wright.

September 18/61
Lanigan, Sask.

Dear Aunty Martha, Mary and Albert,

This will be a very short letter, it is the saddest day of our lives.
Daddy passed away, at the hospital, this morning at 7 a.m. We had stayed with him until 10 last evening. He had no pain, as his left side was paralyzed, if only he had been able to speak to us it would have been a little easier, he tried to tell us so much.

The funeral will be on Thursday the 21st at 2 p.m. We are going to ask the minister to have the hymn "The Day thou gavest is ended", which you mentioned in your last letter. We wondered if he had asked you about it. Dorothy and I will be home with Mom for awhile, she is heartbroken, as we all are. We are so glad that Uncle Sam and Aunty Ada are also with us and the many kind friends.

Our love,
Elsie

John's eldest daughter Elsie Webb wrote this airmail letter to tell her Aunt Martha Ann and family in Bollington of the death of her father John on 18 September 1961.

Acknowledgements

In addition to those mentioned in the Preface and Acknowledgements to 'Letters from a Lady's Maid', many other friends have been involved in this team effort. I would like to sincerely thank everyone who has willingly given their time and various skills at different stages, just when needed.

To Gill Parry and Hazel Weselby for scripting handwritten letters and putting them on to computer, also Kim Brownhill, Nigel Raeburn and Michael Burdekin for advanced computer help. To Alan Chapman whose time and special expertise in setting text and pictures ready for the printer has enabled this book to be published.

To Jean and Stephen Osborne for scripting a selection of handwritten poems and David Fenton, Nigel Raeburn, Cynthia and Peter Jones for scripting handwritten recipes. To Peter Jones who spent time in composing picture pages with captions from the scanned material and who combined additional information with the Tithe Map of 1849

To David Gilligan, editor of North Cheshire Family History Society for advice on a simplified Family Tree and publicity in their magazine. To Roger and Liz de Mercado for help with membership publicity. To John Fielding, Family History Society of Cheshire for scanning additional original material and to Joan Irving for indexing the book.

To Bollington Civic Society Chairman, Tim Boddington whose suggestion to rewrite this longer book in time for the Bollington Festival May 2005 was the catalyst.

To Ken Edwards for publishing advice and to his wife Sandra Edwards for time spent editing the book and to Molly Spink for her advice.

To my family for support, help and encouragement, especially Helene Hein for the information from Canada. To Christine Beard, Philip Wright's granddaughter for her grandmother's letter of September 1890, and for publishing support. To Dr. John Wright for permission to use the informal wedding photograph taken by his grandfather, Isaac Thomas Wright, in chapter 6.

To Thelma Whiston, Jean Ransley, Emily White, Christine Boulding, Chris Connick, Marie Moss and the Gaskell Society for help with publicity and the Discovery Centre, Clarence Mill.

To George Longden for permission to use his postcard of Lowerhouse, To Bollington Civic Society Photographic Archive for the photograph of Lowerhouse School, and to Harold and Sheila Skelhorn for more recent information about the school.

To Bollington Methodist Church for permission to use the 1983 sketch of the church.

Thanks to many other people who have offered their advice and support in various ways.
By working as a team this book has miraculously been made possible so that others can share this unique 'time capsule' of 'Voices from the Past'.

Jean M. Wright 2005

Further Reading and Sources

Bollington Census Returns, 1861 and 1871.

Bollington Ecclesiastical Census 10 March 1851, Cheshire Record Office.

Bollington Tithe Commutation Act Map and Award 28 June 1848, Cheshire Record Office.

Bollington Wesleyan Methodist Church Register and Records. Cheshire Records Office.

Bryant's Map 1831, Cheshire Record Office.

Child Mrs/de Chatelain Madame Girl's Own Book" 1856.

De Dillmont Therese "Encyclopaedia of Needlework".

Flanders, Juliet " The Victorian House" 2002.

Gardiner Juliet "Edwardian County House" 2002.

Greg, Mary & Greg, Amy "Layman's Legacy" 1883.

Groves Sylvia "History of Needlework Tools and Accessories" 1966.

Johnson Eleanor "Needlework Tools" 1978.

Johnson Eleanor "Needlework & Embroidery Tools" 1999.

Johnson Eleanor "Thimbles" 1982.

Linkman, Audrey " The Victorians – Photographic Portraits".

Longden, G & Spink, M "A Factory Community" 1990.

Longden, G & Spink, M "Looking back at Bollington" 1986.

Quarrybank Mill archives: Adam Daber, curator 2003. Information on Samuel Greg, junior, and Lowerhouse.

Prestbury St Peter's Parish Registers.

Taunton, Nerylla "Antique Needlework Tools and Embroideries" 1997.

Trade Directories, Macclesfield Library.

Wright Jean M. "Letters from a Lady's Maid" 2003.

Wright Jean M. "Martha Ann's Story" 1991.

Wright Jean M. "People called Methodists" 1983.

Wright Jean M. "Underhill Family of Macclesfield" 1978.

Wright, Samuel. "Fallen Leaves" a book of his handwritten poems.

Wright Family collection, Macclesfield Museums Trust.

Wright Family original letters, papers, poems and recipes, and 1963 tape recording of Martha Ann Wright deposited at Cheshire Record Office.

Photographs and Illustrations
Colour photographs

Black and white photographs and illustrations

Index

Family Tree Extract

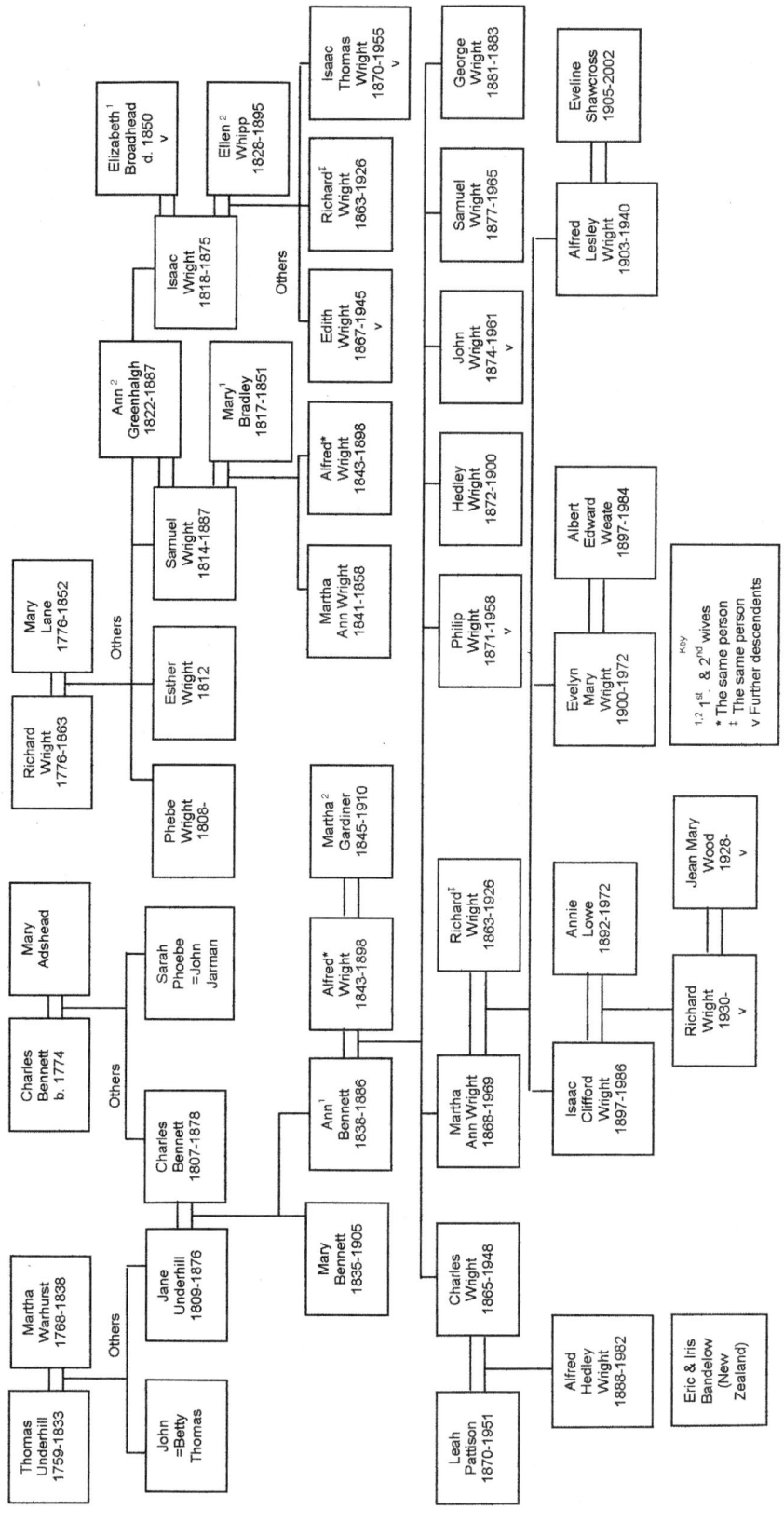

Key
1,2 1st & 2nd wives
* The same person
‡ The same person
v Further descendents